SCOUTS

Volume 15

True Tales of the Old West

by

Charles L. Convis

PIONEER PRESS, CARSON CITY, NEVADA

Library of Congress Catalog Card Number: 96-68502

ISBN 1-892156-05-9 (Volume)
ISBN 0-9651954-0-6 (Series)

Printed by
KNI, Incorporated
Anaheim, California

CONTENTS

STILL ON TOP OF THE GROUND (JOE MILNER)   2
THEM SUCKERS WAS TOUGH (SEMINOLE NEGROES)   5
YOUNG SCOUT IN THE NORTH (GEORGE NORTHRUP)   8
PICTURES IN THE SKY (JACK HART)   10
BITTER VENGEANCE NEAR BITTER SPRINGS (KIT CARSON &
   ALEXIS GODEY)   12
THE BLACK BEAVER   15
ONE DAY OF SCOUTING (WILLIAM FOSTER)   19
NATTY BUMPPO OF KANSAS (WILL COMSTOCK)   20
CLOSE CALLS FOR JACK PEATE   22
A YOUNG SCOUT SEES THE WEST (SIGMUND SCHLESINGER)   25
YOUNG IN YEARS, OLD IN SKILL (JACK STILWELL)   28
OH, FOR A THOUSAND TONGUES TO SING (ALLISON PLILEY &
   JACK DONOVAN)   30
FATHER AND SON (LOUIS AND HUDSON FARLEY)   33
A COMMON GRAVE (GEORGE CULVER & WILLIAM WILSON)   34
MYSTERIOUS HEADDRESS (BARNEY DAY)   35
UNNAMED SCOUT (BEN CLARK)   36
A LITTLE GERMAN RIDES FOR HELP (WILLIAM SCHMALSLE)   38
HEROES HERE HAVE BEEN (AMOS CHAPMAN & BILLY DIXON)   40
HIS FINEST MOMENT (AL SIEBER)   43
THE SIBLEY SCOUT (FRANK GROUARD)   47
A QUIET MAN (CHARLEY REYNOLDS)   50
A SCOUT'S WARNING (MITCH BOUYER)   52
SCOUT AT THE LITTLE BIG HORN (WHITE-MAN-RUNS-HIM)   54
LIFE WAS BORING AWAY FROM THE INDIANS (TOM LeFORGE)   58
FIRST SCALP FOR CUSTER (BUFFALO BILL CODY)   60

ORDERING INFORMATION   62

ILLUSTRATIONS

BLACK BEAVER   17
ALLISON PLILEY   31
FRANK GROUARD   49
WHITE-MAN-RUNS-HIM   55

STILL ON TOP OF THE GROUND

California Joe Milner, named by Custer as chief of scouts for the Washita campaign, was big — six feet two inches, and two hundred pounds. Considered by some the best rifle shot on the plains, he smoked his pipe like a chimney and talked on any subject like an auctioneer. Unfortunately, he also drank a lot — not so much at one time, but there were so many times. His drunken celebration before the Washita Battle got him a quick demotion from Custer.

It's unclear what, if anything, Milner did at that November 27, 1868, battle. He brought the news of Custer's victory to General Sheridan on the morning of the 29th, and Custer's command reached Sheridan at noon on December 1, so Milner may have left before the battle ended.

Sheridan, commanding the follow-up campaign, shared Custer's views of the scout. He described Milner as an "invaluable guide and Indian fighter when liquor was unavailable." But Sheridan kept him as a scout, at least until the morning he was delayed because Milner had got "gloriously tipsy in some mysterious way." Feeling he could not move without Milner, Sheridan waited, but twenty-four hours later the "incorrigible old rascal was still dead drunk." Sheridan stuffed him into an ambulance and hauled him back to Fort Sill.

Moses Embree Milner had quit school at fourteen and disappeared into the Kentucky woods, his rifle on his shoulder. Five years passed before his family saw him again. He trapped in the Rockies and served in the war against Mexico, first as a packer with Stephen W. Kearney, then as a scout for Alexander Doniphan.

After the war, he resumed trapping and then returned home to marry on his twenty first birthday, May 29, 1850. He and his fourteen-year-old bride honeymooned in an emigrant wagon train to California.

After prospecting successfully, Joe moved to Oregon, where he bought a farm and got his lifelong nickname.

But farming was dull, and California Joe ran pack trains to mines, guided a wagon train from St. Joseph to Oregon, and became well acquainted with a young lieutenant fresh out of West Point, Philip H. Sheridan. He also operated a toll road into the Idaho mines.

In 1862, after a long recovery from injuries received in a knife to claw fight with a mountain lion, whose cub Joe was holding in his hand when mother intervened, Milner moved to the new goldfields in Montana Territory. There Joe struck it rich. He had left the mountain lion behind, dead, and that's how he left the claim jumpers who tried to steal his claim. When Montana's famous vigilantes came after him, he struck fear in their hearts, and they never bothered him again.

Joe was in Colorado Territory in 1864, scouting for the army at Fort Lyon. There he saw the Colorado militia in action at Sand Creek, which he deplored, saying, "the cruelties and mutilations practiced by Chivington's men were beyond belief."

Joe went to Santa Fe, where he met Kit Carson and was with him at the First Battle of Adobe Walls. Carson said he never knew a better Indian fighter or a braver man than California Joe. In that battle, Joe's mule was killed under him, and Joe killed several Indians at a very long range.

After prospecting in Colorado, fighting Apaches in New Mexico, and scouting for General Hancock in Kansas, Joe began a close friendship with Wild Bill Hickok. In 1868 he renewed his friendship with Phil Sheridan, now a general.

Custer made California Joe his chief scout as the 7th Cavalry moved south from Fort Dodge, looking for hostile Indians along the Washita River. Joe led the regiment to Black Kettle's camp before he got fired, but he stayed on good terms with Custer. He wrote Custer from California in 1874 that he was "still on top of the ground."

During the 1875-76 winter, Joe went to the Red Cloud Indian Agency at Fort Robinson, Nebraska, and camped for a time on the Niobrara River with his friend, John Richard. They drank heavily, and had many Indians visitors at their camp. After Joe moved on to the Black Hills, Richard was murdered. Moccasin tracks in the snow suggested the work of Indians, but a rumor circulated that Joe was the killer. Joe believed the rumor was started by Tom Newcomb, who had come to the Black Hills gold rush from Oregon. No reason was given for Joe's suspicion; perhaps he and Newcomb had known each other in Oregon.

Three days after Wild Bill Hickok was shot in the back in Deadwood, in August, 1876, Joe reached the town, determined to avenge the killing of his friend. Joe knew the killer was Jack McCall, but when he saw Newcomb carrying a rifle in the street, he grabbed the weapon, saying he would kill Newcomb if he saw him in town again with a gun.

McCall was freed after a farce of a trial by a miner's jury, and Joe followed his trail to Fort Laramie. He learned that McCall had been arrested and was being held for a court trial. The authorities wisely refused to let Joe visit their prisoner. Joe then joined George Crook's expedition as a scout, being discharged at Fort Robinson on October 25. He was ordered to go to Fort Fetterman and scout for Ranald Mackenzie's 4th Cavalry, which was starting a winter expedition against the Cheyennes. But Joe wanted to celebrate for a few days before taking his next job.

On October 29, in a bar at the nearby Red Cloud Agency, a drunken Joe saw Newcomb walk in. Newcomb drew his pistol, but Joe drew faster, and bystanders scattered.

Instead of shooting, Joe said, "Put up your gun, Tom, and join us in a drink."

They shook hands and drank together. They even talked about Richard's murder and the rumor that had spread. Joe thought all trouble was over when he heard Newcomb say, as they parted, "now, Joe, everything is all right."

But a half hour later a shot rang out, and California Joe Milner fell dead. He had been shot in the back by Tom Newcomb, waiting in ambush.

The army held Newcomb for four days. During that time they had to protect him from vigilantes, as they waited for distant civil authorities to arrive. But a blizzard delayed the authorities, and the army had to turn Newcomb loose. He wasted no time getting out of the country.

Based on his long service to the army, California Joe got a military funeral. His bones still lie in a weed-covered, forgotten location in the old Fort Robinson cemetery.

California Joe Milner was an awesome man as he strode across the western landscape, his long frame wrapped in a cavalry overcoat, cavalry pants tucked in to his boots, a giant-sized, slouch hat on his head. His alert eyes, set deep under bushy brows, missed nothing, and his constantly smoking pipe jutted out from an encircling, full beard. No one dared get in his way as he crossed and re-crossed the Old West, trying one thing after another, searching for a challenge equal to the fire burning inside. Bigger that Life? Well, if you created a man from bits and pieces of all the scouts in the Old West, your product could be exactly like California Joe.

Suggested reading: Earle Forrest, *California Joe: Noted Scout and Indian Fighter* (Caldwell, Idaho: Caxton Printers, 1935).

THEM SUCKERS WAS TOUGH

The facts of history can sometimes baffle people who think others can be easily catalogued and their behavior predicted on factors like skin color. Before the Civil War, some Blacks owned other Blacks, and Indians sometimes caught black slaves, returning them to their white owners. The idea that skin color always united people was too simple to be true. After the war, former black slaves joined the army to follow white officers attacking Indians. Four Medal of Honor men, buried in a tiny, rural cemetery in Texas, demonstrate that life is too complicated for simple ideas.

The men, called Seminole Negroes, were descendants of escaped slaves who found sanctuary with the Seminole Indians of Florida. Removed to Indian Territory with the Seminoles, the black men feared kidnapping by Whites followed by a return to slavery, so they escaped to freedom in Mexico in the early 1850s. By this time, some had intermarried with the Seminoles, but those who joined Santa Anna's army looked just like modern Blacks.

Two more decades produced great changes on both sides of the international border, and Indian raids in West Texas brought the frontier army to protect settlers. The Seminole Negroes, homesick for a land now free of slavery, wanted to come back. After twenty years in Catholic Mexico, they were still faithful Baptists, and they missed their native land.

The army offered them jobs as scouts, saying it would transport the men and their families to the United States, give the families provisions and land, and pay the scouts at soldiers' pay. The first group of Seminole Negroes crossed the Rio Grande on July 4, 1870, and ten of them signed up as scouts at Fort Duncan, Texas.

Two things distinguished the scouts from the regular soldiers in the black regiments of the army — language and dress. They spoke Spanish, as well as English, and they spurned regimentation and uniforms. Some even wore feathered headdresses along with the blue pants the army issued them.

In 1871 another group crossed to settle at Fort Clark, near Brackettville, Texas, and twenty of that group signed up as scouts. By 1873 over twenty-five scouts from each group were serving an army, glad to have employed such skilled hunters, trailers, and guides. Then Lieutenant John L. Bullis assumed command of the scouts. He was a tough soldier with experience as a white officer in Black regiments during and after the Civil War.

In May, 1873, Bullis's scouts led Ranald Mackenzie's 4th Cavalry on a raid into Mexico against Apaches, Lipans, and Kickapoos. These Indians had been stealing Texas cattle and crossing the border to avoid pursuit. The Seminoles knew where the Indians hid out, and Mackenzie's raid ended the safe haven the thieves had been enjoying in Mexico.

Bullis was brave and faithful to his men. He led by example, more like a war chief than most army officers. By 1881, he had led the scouts on twenty-five expeditions and had, himself, won four citations for valor in battle.

Adam Payne got his Medal of Honor in September 1874, during the Red River War. Wearing his buffalo-horn headdress, he led three scouts a day's march ahead of Mackenzie's troops. Twenty-five Comanches attacked, and Payne killed at least six of the enemy as he got all his scouts safely back to the troops. A few days later, he led Mackenzie to the Palo Duro Canyon, where the cavalry destroyed fourteen hundred Indian horses and tons of camp equipment and supplies, a devastating blow to the hostiles with winter coming on.

The other three scouts got their Medals of Honor the next April as they rode with Bullis pursuing hostiles who had stolen seventy-five horses. John Ward, Isaac Payne, and

Pompey Factor were the only scouts Bullis took, as he wanted to travel fast and leave little trail.

Near the mouth of the Pecos River, they ran into a dismounted party of thirty Comanches armed with repeating rifles. These weren't the thieves, but the scouts couldn't resist the fight, so they dismounted, crept up on the enemy, and attacked. Forty-five minutes later, with three Indians killed, the scouts decided to withdraw. They reached their horses, but Bullis' horse was so excited he couldn't be mounted.

"Boys, we can't leave him," John Ward shouted.

Isaac Payne and Pompey Factor kept up their fire to hold back the advancing Comanches while Ward scooped Bullis up behind him onto Ward's horse. Ward barely escaped alive. One bullet pierced his gun sling and another shattered the stock, as the men dashed through the Comanches and got away.

During their twelve-year history, the Seminole Negro scouts never lost a man. "Divine providence," they said.

But God was kinder than the Texas citizens. The army never had the land to give to the Negro Seminoles as it promised, so the Blacks planted their gardens and cultivated their small fields on the military reservations. The army didn't complain, but the Texans did. "Just squatters, with no rights at all," they said.

On May 19, 1876, Chief John Horse and Titus Payne were fired on by Texas citizens, irate at the trespassing on the military reservations. Payne was killed instantly and Chief John Horse wounded.

On January 1, 1877, Adam Payne, wanted for assault, was at a dance when the sheriff arrived. Instead of making an arrest, the sheriff crept up behind Payne and fired his shotgun into Payne's back from so close the muzzle blast set the dying man's clothing on fire.

Descendants of the Seminole Negroes still live along Las Moras Creek, southwest of Brackettville. Nearby is the little cemetery where lie four Medal of Honor men.

One of those descendants, Willie Warrior who knew his history, accurately referred to the scouts when he said, "Them suckers was tough."

Suggested reading: Frank N. Schubert, *Black Valor* (Wilmington: Scholarly Resources, 1984).

YOUNG SCOUT IN THE NORTH

Gerrit Smith, famous abolitionist, reformer, and philanthropist, may have seen something unusual in his sixteen-year-old New York neighbor when the boy left to go west, so he gave George Northrup his blessing. George walked 2500 miles to St. Paul that 1853 summer and found work as a clerk in A. L. Larpenteur's fur trading post. But clerking was dull. By September George had a new rifle and revolver and was on his way to Pembina (on the Red River in present North Dakota) with five Indian and half breed companions. He expected to be back soon with a dog sled full of furs, but he stayed to teach at the mission school, replacing a man who had been killed by hostile Sioux.

George already had a good education, including latin, and he studied the Ojibwa language as he taught Ojibwa, Cree, and Assiniboine children. George was a nice looking young man, five feet nine, one hundred sixty pounds. He let his auburn hair grow down below his shoulders. He wore a blue Hudson's Bay coat with white moleskin pants and a large knife stuck into a scabbard held by the red sash around his waist. He called it his half breed costume. George didn't smoke or chew and never drank to excess. His speech was so pure that some rough frontier characters wondered at first if he was a woman in disguise.

George had a dream. He wanted to travel through the Indian tribes all the way to the Bering Strait, and then cross Asia and Europe to reach civilization by going west. He was well read, having a personal library of 150 volumes when he was back in St. Paul in 1855, working in a bookstore.

Very likely George was influenced by French author René de Chateaubriand. The Frenchman, impressed by Rousseau's idea of the noble savage, had been to New York, where he tramped through Indian country to Niagara Falls. Then he wrote *Les Natchez,* a novel praised by Rousseau and probably devoured by George Northrup.

George wrote home in April, 1855. "Have packed up my books. Am studying mathematics and navigation. You will probably hear from me at some point in the Rocky Mountains."

Then the eighteen-year-old set out to the west on foot with a handcart and a dog for company. He had been offered thirty dollars a month to guide an expedition into the north shore of Lake Superior, but that was not the direction George cared about.

George had gone on a buffalo hunt the year before. He

went far enough west then to see the Missouri River, probably from the coteau du Missouri, south of the Souris River. In 1855 he followed the 1853 trail of Isaac Stevens, who had been looking for a railroad route to the Pacific.

George trudged along for thirty-six days, seeing no one, hearing no voice but his own. Then he woke one morning to find that everything in his handcart had been stolen by Indians. Disappointed that his expedition had ended so soon, George retreated to Big Stone Lake, living on frogs for four days. By the end of July he had been hired to teach Sisseton Sioux farming skills at the head of the Minnesota River.

George thought about buying land and settling down. He wrote his mother in 1856 for authority, as the oldest child in the family, to pre-empt land at Shakopee, near St. Paul. Nothing came of that.

In 1857 he sent three men, with horses and equipment, to cut hay and build a trading post at Devil's Lake. They were killed by hostile Indians.

In 1859 George mapped a stage road from St. Paul to the Red River and guided the first stages over the route. By then he was considered the Kit Carson of the Northwest. In the 1860-1861 winter he carried mail by dog sled between Fort Abercrombie and Pembina.

When the Civil War started, George enlisted at Fort Snelling and was assigned to the Fifth Iowa Cavalry. By 1863 he was the first sergeant of his company, fighting in Virginia. General George Crook made George one of the scouts in his division.

When George re-enlisted, the three Minnesota companies in the regiment were sent back to Fort Snelling to protect the frontier. In 1864, they marched west and joined Alfred Sully's column marching up the Missouri River.

On July 11, at the future site of Fort Rice, George wrote a friend that they expected to meet hostile Sioux about one hundred and fifty miles north. "This may be the last letter you will receive from me."

His distance estimate was right, and so was his premonition. On July 28, 1864, Sully's two thousand soldiers fought about eight thousand Indians. Only two soldiers were killed, but one of them was 27-year-old George Northrup, a fine young scout in the north.

Suggested reading: Gertrude W. Ackermann, "George Northrup, Frontier Scout," in *Minnesota History, v. 19* (December, 1938).

PICTURES IN THE SKY

Mirages are common in the West. Objects below the horizon become visible when light bends as it crosses temperature boundaries. If the air forms a lens, the image will be enlarged and sometimes inverted. Custer's command marching into the sky in 1876 was a famous mirage. Nine years earlier a mirage in Kansas saved the lives of two people.

Susie Raume's widowed father had settled in the Elkhorn River Valley, fifteen miles north of Fort Harker. He could look up from his cabin to the Twin Mounds, low peaks dominating the ridge that separated the Elkhorn Valley from the valley to the south. Eighteen-year-old Susie helped her father care for four younger brothers and sisters. Dark-haired, modest, and gentle, Susie was quite pretty.

Jack Hart, about twenty-three and brave as a lion, scouted for the army out of Fort Harker. In April 1867 a 5th Cavalry company, with Jack scouting, stopped at the Raume ranch for a noontime halt. Susie and Jack fell instantly in love.

For the next few weeks, Jack's horse wore out the trail between Fort Harker and the ranch. Within a month Jack and Susie were engaged. Then, a detachment of the 7th Cavalry took a disappointed Jack out on a short campaign.

"We'll marry as soon as I'm back," Jack promised.

"I'll be waiting," Susie said.

When he returned from the scout, Jack bought a new suit, got cleaned up and shaved, and he was ready to ride north.

But the fort commander sent him northwest to meet a detachment of the 5th Cavalry, coming in from the Platte. Downhearted, Jack rode out to meet the soldiers.

He found the soldiers right away. When they camped that afternoon, Jack realized that he was only fifteen miles west of the Raume ranch. He got permission to ride to it.

"I'll be back first thing in the morning," Jack said.

When he rode into the Elkhorn Valley at sunset, he saw smoke rising from the corrals. He cried when he found the scalped bodies of Susie's father and the four younger children at the smoldering cabin.

But where was Susie? At first Jack groaned, thinking the Indians had carried her away to a life worse than death. He looked around, afraid to hope but unable to not hope. Then he heard the moans from the spring. He found Susie there, stabbed in the chest but still alive.

Jack dressed the wound. He made Susie comfortable and stayed awake with her all night. When the sun shone on the Twin Mounds, Susie woke. Her fever had dropped. If Jack could just get her on his horse he could take her to the doctor at Fort Harker.

"Let's try, Jack," she said, her voice weak.

"I should take a look first, up on the ridge. Make sure the Indians are gone. I'll leave the carbine here, by you, Susie. I'll be back in ten minutes."

When Jack came out of the timber near the top of the ridge, he saw the cougar. Normally the animal would have run. But this one was surprised, and she had three small kittens with her. She pounced on Jack.

Her claws had gouged deeply into Jack's shoulder before he could draw his knife. During the short, furious battle, Jack was clawed and ripped, but he killed the cougar. His torn body, drenched with blood, collapsed when the cougar died.

Fifth Cavalry troopers were grooming their horses and enjoying the fresh summer morning, when an officer suddenly pointed to the Twin Mounds. The peaks loomed up blue and clear with the rising sunlight behind them. Above the ridge, upside down, two figures moved against the sky.

"Look men, a mirage," the officer said.

The officer got his field glasses and watched, spellbound. He saw a celestial apparition of a man and a beast, engaged in a deadly struggle. The soldiers stopped working to watch the curious panorama in the sky.

"Looks like our scout," the officer said. "Can't make out what kind of animal it is."

In a few minutes the sun was higher, and the mirage disappeared. The officer led his troops to the ridge to see if they were needed. It was a four hour ride.

They found Jack and the cougar, lying together. The troops had a surgeon with them.

"The scout's still alive," the surgeon said.

When Jack could, he told them about Susie. They found her, still feverish, wondering what had happened to her lover.

Two years passed before Susie was well enough to marry. Jack became a prosperous rancher, and they raised a large family.

Suggested reading: Henry Inman, *Tales of the Trail* (Topeka: Clark & Company, 1898).

BITTER VENGEANCE NEAR BITTER SPRINGS

Explorer John C. Fremont said that his scouts, Alexis Godey and Kit Carson, would have both been field marshals if they had served in Napoleon's army. Godey, born of French parents in St. Louis, was closely associated with Kit Carson, and they both served as scouts on three of Fremont's expeditions. Godey's fame began in April 1844, during the second expedition.

On March 24, 1844, Fremont said goodbye to Captain John Sutter and started his return east. With Godey and Carson scouting ahead, Fremont headed southeast down the San Joaquin Valley. He had just made a hair-raising crossing of the rugged Sierras to get into California, and he planned to go south in search of a lower pass discovered ten years before by Joseph Walker.

The party crossed the Cosumnes, Mokelumne, Calaveras, and Stanislaus Rivers, camping on the Merced on April 1. While local Indians guided, the scouts watched the country carefully, prepared to ward off any Indian attack. The party continued up the San Joaquin River until it turned east into the mountains. They followed along the foothills and crossed the mountains at Oak Creek Pass on April 14.

The expedition descended into a dry region of Yucca trees where local Indians warned them that their animals would perish from thirst if they continued east. Fremont took their advice and bore further south to intersect the Old Spanish Trail. This was a pack mule route from Los Angeles running northeast past present Las Vegas and looping through Utah and Colorado to Santa Fe.

They reached the trail on April 20 where it crossed the Mohave River. Knowing of the waterless stretches ahead, Fremont ordered a one-day halt to rest the stock. This camp was about twelve miles southwest of present Barstow, California.

By the twenty-third, the Mohave River had disappeared into the sandy desert; the next day they killed three of the weakest cattle and dried the meat for later consumption. On the following afternoon they met two Mexicans coming down the trail, Andreas Fuentes and Pablo Hernandez, a boy of eleven. They had been part of a group of six who were driving a herd of thirty horses up the trail. About eighty miles on ahead, at the Archilette camping ground (now called Resting Springs), they had been attacked by about a hundred

Indians. Fuentes' wife, Pablo's parents, and the other herder were all believed killed. Fuentes and Pablo were on mounted guard at the time and had escaped, driving part of their herd ahead. They had left that remnant of the herd at Bitter Springs and had ridden on ahead on their own mounts.

Early on April 25 Fremont's expedition, with Fuentes and Pablo now added, reached Bitter Springs. To no one's surprise, the stolen horses were not to be found. Godey and Carson, after thinking hard about the attack on Fuentes' wife and both of the boy's parents, said they wanted to ride on ahead and see if they could recover the horses and punish some Indians. Fremont gave his permission, saying the expedition would remain in camp at Bitter Springs until the scouts returned.

After a thirty-hour, wild ride covering a hundred miles of waterless desert, Godey and Carson galloped back into Bitter Springs. They were driving stolen horses ahead of them, and Godey brandished his gun in triumph. Here is what Fremont wrote about Godey's most famous exploit:

"A war-whoop was heard, such as Indians make when returning from a victorious enterprise; and soon Carson and Godey appeared, driving before them a band of horses, recognized by Fuentes to be part of those they had lost. Two bloody scalps, dangling from the end of Godey's gun, announced that they had overtaken the Indians as well as the horses."

Godey and Carson had followed the trail into a narrow defile and slept there from midnight until dawn. After riding forward a short distance, they found the Indian camp.

"Giving the war-shout, they instantly charged into the camp, regardless of the number which the *four* lodges would imply. The Indians received them with a flight of arrows shot from their longbows, one of which passed through Godey's shirt-collar, barely missing the neck."

The scouts had fired, dropping two Indians; the rest had escaped except for a small boy whom they captured. They scalped the two fallen Indians, but one of them leaped to his feet with a hideous howl, blood streaming from his skinned head.

"An old squaw, possibly his mother, stopped and looked back from the mountainside she was climbing, threatening and lamenting. The frightful spectacle appalled the stout hearts of our men; but they did what humanity required, and quickly terminated the agonies of the gory savage."

The scouts released their boy captive, gathered up about fifteen of the stolen horses, and started down the trail to return to Fremont's camp.

"The time, place, object, and numbers considered," Fremont continued, "this expedition of Carson and Godey may be considered among the boldest which the annals of western adventure, so full of daring deeds, can present. Two men, in a savage desert, pursue day and night an unknown body of Indians into the defiles of an unknown mountain — attack them on sight, without counting numbers — and defeat them in an instant — and for what? To punish the robbers of the desert, and to avenge the wrongs of Mexicans whom they did not know. I repeat: it was Carson and Godey who did this — the former an American, born in Boonslick county of Missouri; the latter a Frenchman, born in St. Louis — and both trained to western enterprise from early life."

When the expedition reached Archilette they found the corpses of the two men the Indians had killed. The women were nowhere to be seen. The corpse of Pedro's father had both legs and one hand cut off. A small dog belonging to Pedro's family had stayed by the corpses, and was overjoyed to see his young master.

"Pedro, poor child, was frantic with grief , and filled the air with lamentations for his father and mother. *Mi Padre! Mi Madre!* — was his incessant cry. When we beheld this pitiable sight, and pictured to ourselves the fate of the two women, carried off by savages so brutal and loathsome, all compunction for the scalped-alive Indian ceased."

Alexis Godey had become a mountain man at age seventeen when he trapped with Jim Bridger and Kit Carson. He and Carson served again as scouts with Fremont's third and fourth expeditions. Godey was the hero of the rescue of the snowbound survivors in the fourth expedition.

Godey served as a lieutenant in the California Battalion, fighting the Mexican Army in 1846. Later he had a sheep ranch near Bakersfield. In 1889, when he was seventy years old, he got too close to a lion in a Los Angeles circus, was scratched severely, and died from blood poisoning. He is buried in Bakersfield, not a long way from the place where he first became famous.

Suggested reading: Col. J. C. Fremont, *The Exploring Expedition to the Rocky Mountains, Oregon, and California* (Buffalo: Derby, Orton & Mulligan, 1854).

THE BLACK BEAVER

His Delaware Indian name was Se-Ket-Tu-Ma-Qua (The Black Beaver); whites usually just said Black Beaver. His knowledge of the country and its Indian tribes, and his intelligence, good judgment, and bravery made him the premier Indian scout from the opening of the West until his death in 1880. In nearly every one of the early transcontinental expeditions, military or scientific, he was the most trusted and intelligent scout. His skill and faithfulness, both to the army and to the early pioneers, helped push the American frontier steadily westward.

Black Beaver spread his blankets on the Missouri, the Columbia, the Rio Grande, the Gila, and the Colorado, but his service on the Staked Plains of West Texas best illustrates the man.

In 1849 Captain Randolph Marcy, with Black Beaver scouting, had led troops out of Fort Smith escorting about five hundred gold rush emigrants through hostile Comanche and Kiowa territory as far as Santa Fe. There, Marcy turned south to Texas and then back northeast, searching out locations for forts to protect future travelers. Black Beaver would eventually locate most of those forts, but his services in decoding a ghastly crime showed his incredible ability.

On October 6, Marcy camped on a small creek, somewhere near present Big Spring, Texas. The next forenoon, Lt. Montgomery Pike Harrison, grandson of the ninth U. S. president and older brother of the future twenty-third, rode out to inspect the trail ahead. He had not returned by dark.

Marcy sent another lieutenant and Black Beaver out to search the next morning. They found Harrison's body, scalped and stripped, lying on some rocks in a ravine. Black Beaver studied the evidence and told Marcy what had happened. Here is Marcy's account of what the scout learned from the clues: "The murder was committed by two Kiowas. They had two mules and one horse with them. They came down upon their victim at full gallop, but finding that he was not disposed to flee, but on the contrary walked his horse towards them, they also pulled up to a walk. The parties met and rode a short distance together, then dismounted, and seating themselves on the grass, smoked together. Here they got possession of his rifle, on pretense as supposed, of examining it. As this was the only weapon he had with him, they then overpowered him, tied him, and placing him upon his horse, led the horse between them into some timber, skirting a ravine, where one falling behind, shot him in the back of his head, the ball found in the brain, indicating that the deed was committed with his own rifle. Hastily stripping him, they scalped him, threw his body into a ravine, and taking everything but one boot and his saddle, made their escape. Some miles farther they halted, and lighting a fire, they prepared some meat for cooking, as the raw meat was found spitted and the fire smoldering. They left here very hastily, as a pair of moccasins, a lariat, and some other articles were dropped in their hurry, occasioned doubtless by hearing the report of the howitzer which was fired from camp at sundown as a guide to the missing officer."

Black Beaver's report was substantiated in all details when the murderers were found.

Harrison was the only casualty on Marcy's long expedition through hostile Indians. The scout's fluency in Comanche and Kiowa and his ability to communicate was credited for that success, but the killing of Harrison was done in secret, something Black Beaver could not prevent. The scout was fluent in eight Indian languages, as well as English, Spanish, and French.

Black Beaver worked another season for Captain Marcy. Much of the captain's success and reputation as a pathfinder in the Southwest was due to Black Beaver. In his book, *The Prairie Traveler,* Marcy said he always found the scout "perfectly reliable, brave, and competent. His reputation as a resolute, determined, and fearless warrior did not admit of question, yet I have never seen a man who wore his laurels with less vanity."

Marcy also mentioned Black Beaver's description of his marriage:

"One time me catch 'um wife. I pay that woman, his modder, one hoss — one saddle — one bridle — two plug tobacco, and plenty goods. I take him home to my house — got plenty meat — plenty corn — plenty everything. One time me go to take walk, maybe so three, maybe so two hours. When I come home that woman he say, 'Black Beaver, what for you go away long time?' I say, 'I not go nowhere. I just take one littel walk.' Then that woman he get heap mad, and say, 'No, Black Beaver, you not take no littel walk. I know what for you go way. You go see nodder woman.' I say, 'Maybe not.' Then that woman cry long time, and all e'time now he mad. You never seen 'Merican woman that a-way?" Marcy replied that he thought women were pretty much alike all over the world.

Black Beaver had commanded a company of Delaware and Shawnee scouts in the war against Mexico, and was called captain by the army from then on. When the army abandoned

BLACK BEAVER

Courtesy, National Archives

Camp Arbuckle in Indian Territory in 1851, it gave the land to the scout, and he developed a fine farm there, sharing the land with other Delaware Indians.

In 1853 Lt. A. W. Whipple asked Black Beaver to scout for him on an expedition he was leading to the Pacific Coast. He described the scout as a meager-looking man of middle size, his long black hair framing a face that was clever, but which bore a melancholy expression of sickness and sorrow. The old scout, now forty-seven, responded to Whipple's request:

"Seven times have I seen the Pacific Ocean at various points; I have accompanied the Americans in three wars, and I have brought home more scalps from my hunting expeditions than one of you could lift. I should like to see the salt water for the eighth time; but I am sick — you offer me more money than has ever been offered to me before — but I am sick. If I die I should like to be buried by my own people."

Whipple stayed three days, trying to convince Black Beaver, and finally went on without him. It seemed to Whipple that each time Black Beaver was almost persuaded, his wife, who sat nearby playing with their son and a bear cub, spoke to him in Delaware, and Black Beaver again declined to go.

In 1861, when Colonel W. H. Emory learned that large numbers of rebels were approaching, he asked Black Beaver to guide his troops from Forts Smith, Cobb, and Arbuckle so they could evade the rebels and reach Fort Leavenworth. The faithful scout abandoned his forty-acre fenced farm with 600 cattle, 300 hogs, horses, mules, implements and equipment, as well as his four-room, hewed log house to once again serve his country.

By 1872 Black Beaver was again farming on the False Washita River near where he had abandoned his earlier farm, and he was living comfortably with cultivated fields and substantial buildings. In October that year he was part of a delegation of plains Indians that traveled to New York and Washington.

Four years later the intrepid scout was baptized in a creek and later he became a Baptist minister. In May, 1880, aged seventy-four, he died suddenly of a heart attack.

Suggested reading: Grant Foreman, *Marcy & the Gold Seekers* (Norman: Univ. of Oklahoma Press, 1939).

ONE DAY OF SCOUTING

On July 3, 1877, after his attack on Looking Glass' camp of Nez Perce, Captain Stephen Whipple of the 1st Cavalry sent two civilians out on a scout. Charles Blewett, twenty-two, and William Foster, twenty-four, struck out for Craig's Ferry on the Salmon River, near present Cottonwood, Idaho. Whipple suspected that Chief Joseph had swum his warriors across near there, and he wanted to know how many and where they were. The scouts never got there.

As Blewett and Foster unknowingly approached Joseph's main camp, Red Spy, a warrior on guard, shot and killed Blewett. Foster raced back to Whipple's troop.

Whipple ordered a ten-man squad under Lieutenant Sevier M. Rains to ride back immediately with Foster. They were to scout the strength and position of the hostiles, and rescue Blewett if he were still alive.

Unknown to Foster, Red Spy had pursued him far enough to see the cavalry camp. He raced back to the Indian camp with the news that the soldiers were close by.

War leaders Rainbow, Two Moons, and Five Wounds led an attack party out at once. When they saw the cavalry tents, they dismounted and quickly prepared for battle. They unwrapped their medicine bundles while softly singing their war songs. The Indians remounted and rode forward to find Lieutenant Rains' command coming in their direction.

The warriors charged the soldiers, shooting six dead in their saddles. The other six whirled, galloped up a hill, and tried to make a stand among some rocks. The Indians dropped out of sight into a ravine and started quietly circling around.

When one of the warriors, Strong Eagle, exposed himself as a decoy to draw the army fire, the rest slipped up behind the whites and killed them all.

With thirteen enemies killed (eleven soldiers and two scouts) and no Indians harmed, the Nez Perce did not ride on to attack Whipple's troop. Satisfied with the day's results, they withdrew to their own camp.

Suggested reading: Alvin M, Josephy, Jr., *The Nez Perce Indians and the Opening of the Northwest* (New Haven: Yale University Press, 1965).

NATTY BUMPPO OF KANSAS

James Fenimore Cooper didn't live long enough to see his wilderness hero, Natty Bumppo, come to life as one of his own relatives. It was Will Comstock, born in 1842 in Comstock, Michigan, a town founded by his father. His mother was Cooper's niece. The young boy probably relished his famous relative's stories of brave frontiersmen and noble savages. At eighteen, Comstock became an Indian trader at Cottonwood Springs, Nebraska. Very friendly with the Cheyenne and Arapaho tribes, he saved the life of a snake-bitten Arapaho. After that, the Indians called him Medicine Bill.

Comstock was first hired as a scout in 1865. After a brief period at Fort Halleck, Wyoming, he joined Troop M of the 2nd Cavalry in western Kansas. When Fort Wallace was built, he moved there to scout for the 7th Cavalry.

Myles Keogh, commanding I Company at the fort, recommended Will to George Custer, saying, "He is an eccentric genius and ardent admirer of everything reckless and daring."

Will scouted for Custer and General Hancock on their 1867 expedition, and he discovered the remains of the Lyman Kidder party. Using his skills of observation and frontier experience, he worked out what had happened in that disaster. Theodore Davis of *Harper's Weekly* was on the expedition, and he described Will as "quiet and unassuming in manner, small in build but compact and sinewy; one of the best riders on the plains, with which he is more familiar than any other white man who roams over them."

Custer wrote: "No Indian knew the country more thoroughly than did Comstock. He was perfectly familiar with every divide, water course, and strip of timber for hundreds of miles in any direction. He knew the dress and peculiarities of every Indian tribe and spoke the languages of many of them. Perfect in horsemanship, fearless in manner, a splendid hunter, and a gentleman by instinct, he was as modest and assuming as he was brave."

When Custer's wagon train went back to Fort Wallace for supplies, Will guided it through the hostile Indians. On June 26, Cheyennes attacked the train, giving the first demonstration of the encircling attack that has since been copied in thousands of movies. Will Comstock was the hero of the defense in that three-hour battle. He emptied many Cheyenne saddles and shouted taunts and insults whenever the Indians turned away.

There is a report — not well substantiated — that Will Comstock entered a buffalo-shooting contest with William Cody to see who was entitled to the name, Buffalo Bill. Cody is reputed to have won the eight-hour hunt in 1867, killing sixty-nine to Comstock's forty-six. At any rate, Cody was the only man on the plains called Buffalo Bill after that.

By summer 1868, central and western Kansas was aflame with hostile Indians. General Phil Sheridan took command and tried to control the hostiles through the influence of scouts whom they knew and trusted. He sent Comstock and Abner (Sharp) Grover to Turkey Leg's Cheyenne camp on Walnut Creek. They had been friends of the chief, and had lived in his camps. Sheridan and the scouts all recognized the risk, given the Indians' growing belligerence but they hoped traditional Indian hospitality toward old friends would keep the scouts safe.

On Saturday, August 15, 1868, the scouts left Fort Hays, hoping to move undetected through the hostiles and slip unseen into Turkey Leg's camp, where they would seek sanctuary in his personal lodge. They reached the camp safely the next day but were surprised at their cool reception. Neither food nor pipe smoking were offered.

The scouts knew that Captain Benteen of the 7th Cavalry was in the field, seeking retaliation for Indian depredations against settlers, and they learned in the village that some its warriors were out looking for the soldiers. When the Indians returned that evening, the cool reception quickly turned icy cold.

The scouts were abruptly told to leave, under an escort of seven warriors. Since they had no choice, they rode out of the camp. Their guards proclaimed their complete friendship with the scouts, but suddenly some of them dropped back and fired their rifles at the scouts' backs. Will Comstock was killed instantly, one bullet entering his brain, another his heart.

Grover, wounded in the back, slipped off his horse and fell to the ground. He lay motionless, feigning death. The Indians, thinking both scouts had been killed, returned to their village.

Grover stayed hidden in the grass all night and all the next day. When darkness came Monday, he slipped away and reached the tracks of the Kansas Pacific, where a passing train took him to Fort Wallace.

At great risk to their lives, Comstock and Grover had tried to prevent a war that would be disastrous to whites and Indians, alike. Will Comstock lost, and his unrecovered body remained on the plains he loved so well.

Suggested reading: John S. Gray, "Will Comstock, Scout: The Natty Bumppo of Kansas," in *Montana, the Magazine of Western History v.* XX, No. 3, July, 1970.

CLOSE CALLS FOR JACK PEATE

Twenty-year-old Jack Peate, son of a Pennsylvania preacher, had run away from home at fifteen to fight Indians. When General Phil Sheridan decided that he needed a force of civilian scouts to protect the Kansas frontier against Indians, he asked Jack for help. Jack had already been scouting for the army, and Sheridan considered him "one of our most trusted and efficient scouts." Jack personally recruited about a fourth of the scouts, but he missed the Battle of Beecher Island that made them famous. He did, however, have three close calls. Hostile Indians had turned Kansas into an inferno that summer of 1868. Jack and seven of his recruits reached Fort Harker a few hours after Major George Forsyth, commanding the scouts, had marched out. Jack and his men were sent on to Fort Hays. There they took the train to the end of track at Sheridan and rode twenty more miles to reach Fort Wallace in western Kansas.

Too late again, Jack learned that Forsyth had led his scouts out of Fort Wallace thirty-six hours before. Jack prevailed upon Colonel Henry Bankhead, post commander, to let him catch up with Forsyth and his command — Lieutenant Fred Beecher, army surgeon Dr. John H. Mooers, and forty-nine scouts. Bankhead even agreed to add nine more scouts from his fort to give Peate's small band more protection against Indians.

But Sheridan refused to let seventeen men ride out into that maelstrom of hostile Indians. "They won't have a chance," Sheridan said. Jack's first close call.

A few days later, on September 21, Captain Louis Carpenter led Company H of the 10th Cavalry out on patrol, and Jack and his scouts — now sixteen — were allowed to go along. Two days after that, four soldiers from Fort Wallace brought dispatches to Carpenter that two of Forsyth's men, Jack Stilwell and Pierre Trudeau, had come in saying that Forsyth had been attacked by hundreds of Indians and was under siege. Bankhead said he was moving out immediately, and Carpenter was also to ride to Forsyth's relief, somewhere west of the forks of the Republican River.

Forsyth had sent Stilwell and Trudeau out for help on the first night of the siege. Two nights later, September 19, he sent out two more, Jack Donovan and A. J. Pliley. The last two reached a ranch and caught a stage to Fort Wallace, arriving after Bankhead left. Pliley then struck out for a detachment of the 2nd Cavalry, patrolling out of Fort Sedgwick, and Donovan, with four local volunteers, headed north to overtake Carpenter.

On September 24 Carpenter's patrol began seeing dead horses and Indians — all killed by gunshot wounds. They knew they were near the place of the siege. Just before the next dawn, they saw five mounted men, Jack Donovan and his four companions.

Donovan told Carpenter that Forsyth's embattled scouts were about twenty miles north. The Captain took fifteen soldiers, the scouts, now numbering twenty-two, and his surgeon, Dr. Jenkins Fitzgerald, and hurried on. They reached the place of the siege, that evening. Jack Peate, riding on ahead, was the first to reach his comrades. He wrote: "Crowned king nor conquering general ne'er received so royal and hearty a welcome as I did when I rode into that island among those staunch-hearted men who lifted me from my horse, embraced me and, strong men though they were, wept, as cheer upon cheer arose. . . . All had that wolfish haggard look which indicates hunger. A terrible stench from the dead horses filled the air."

Lt. Beecher, Dr. Mooers, and three scouts were dead. Forsyth and about half the surviving scouts had been wounded. Forsyth had been shot three times. Fitzgerald wanted to amputate his leg, but Forsyth refused.

The survivors had been living for nine days on putrid meat cut from their dead horses. They had learned that sprinkling gunpowder on the meat reduced the offensive odor. The attacking Indians had only recently moved out. Carpenter first moved the survivors to a clean place a half mile away, where the stench was not so bad, and Doctor Fitzgerald could begin his work. Doctor Mooers, shot early in the battle, had not been able to do anything for the wounded. The dead were re-buried deeper to get their bodies away from wolves.

Colonel Bankhead arrived the next day. Stilwell and Trudeau were with him, along with two companies of the 2nd Cavalry which had joined Bankhead after Pliley found them. The following day, Sunday the 27th, the entire command moved a short distance to the area where Carpenter had made his last camp before finding Forsyth. Here Peate and other scouts found a live Indian and killed him. Then they saw three horses in the distance, and decided to capture them. But four Indians jumped up from some bushes and ran to the horses. Three mounted and escaped into a ravine. Peate decided after their scouting the next day, that they would have certainly been ambushed if they had followed. Jack's second close call.

While the mounted scouts chased the fourth Indian on foot, Trudeau shot him in the leg. The Indian — on the ground now — calmly raised his revolver and fired it five times at his pursuers before it misfired. He was chanting his death song as the scouts ran up and finished him off. The Indian's revolver had not fired the sixth time because a bullet from Donovan's pistol had jammed into the revolving magazine, rendering it useless. Jack Peate's third close call.

The next morning, before moving out, Peate rode up to where they had left the body of the Indian they had killed. He wrote that wolves had come down for a banquet, and only the bones were left.

In months to come Indians would admit that they had lost at least seventy-five killed in the battle, with over two hundred wounded. The scouts' losses were five dead and about thirty wounded. Two months later an army patrol found an Indian village camped at the site of the battle. Chasing them away, they found that the graves of Lieutenant Frederick Beecher (nephew of Henry Ward Beecher, America's famous clergyman), Doctor Mooers, and one scout were empty.

It took Major Forsyth two years to recover from his injuries, but he saved his leg. The head wound gave him severe headaches for the rest of his life. He died in 1915, two months short of his seventy-eighth birthday.

Suggested reading: James J. Peate, "J. J. Peate Tells of the Relief" in Simon Matson (ed.) *The Beecher Island Annual* (September, 1960.)

A YOUNG SCOUT SEES THE WEST

Sigmund Schlesinger, a Jewish boy, emigrated from Hungary to New York in 1864, when he was fifteen. A year later he left his family to go west, seeking adventure. He delivered newspapers in Hays City, Kansas, where his customers included General Custer and Wild Bill Hickok. He also washed dishes, tended bar, tried to start a bakery with six dollars capital, hauled wood, hunted coyotes, and night-herded mules.

He was still looking for adventure when he learned that Major George Forsyth was organizing a 50-man band of scouts to help the army fight Indians. It sounded exciting, so Sigmund asked his friend, Jack Stilwell, if he thought Forsyth would take him.

"I'm joining," Jack said. "Lieutenant Beecher will be the major's right hand man, and he knows me well. I'll put in a good word for you."

"We don't need more boys," Beecher said. "We need tough old buffalo men."

But Sig's persistence impressed Beecher and Forsyth, who finally said, "Oh, hell, Beecher, sign him up."

Sig remembered a rough old muleskinner, standing nearby, who heard Forsyth and interjected, "he'll be a-hollerin' fer his ma fust time he sees a redskin."

"I was not used to the saddle," Sig wrote. "My revolvers and saddle bags were always where they should not have been. My bridle arm became stiff and lame; every bone in my body ached. The ride and the day seemed never to end. I was chafed by the saddle and some parts became swollen to twice their normal size."

But Sig Schlesinger took good care of his horse and followed orders faithfully. Forsyth said the boy "proved himself a gallant soldier among brave men."

On September 16 the scouts camped on Arickaree Creek, a small branch of the Republican River, just west of the Colorado-Kansas boundary. That night they finished eating their rations, as they intended to live on game for the rest of their expedition.

At dawn seven hundred Indians attacked. They were the warriors in one Northern Cheyenne village, two Sioux villages (Oglala and Brule), and a few Arapahoes. Many of the Indians were in the Dog Soldier Society, and their illustrious medicine man, Roman Nose, was present but reluctant to participate because he had broken a taboo and didn't have time for the purification ceremony that would restore his invincibility. The scouts ran to a low, sandy island in the shallow stream, tied their horses to bushes and scrubby cottonwood trees, and used their bare hands, cups, plates, and knives to scoop out entrenchments in the sand. Within an hour, all their horses were killed, as were Lieutenant Beecher and two scouts. Dr. Mooers mortally wounded with a shot to his head, lingered three days before he died, but he was unable to provide anyone medical help. About half of the scouts were wounded. Major Forsyth, the first one hit, had been shot three times, once in each leg and in the head.

Young school teacher Frank Harrington had two wounds that were remembered by the survivors for years afterward. First, an arrow hit his head, the steel point driving into the bone above his left eye. Even though the butt of the point was still visible, George Clark, fighting next to Harrington, could not pull the arrow out. Harrington continued to fight with the arrow sticking out of his head. Later that day he was shot in the head, the bullet striking the butt of the arrow point at such an angle that it knocked the arrow to the ground. Blood from both wounds annoyed Harrington as it ran into his eyes, but he kept fighting and survived the battle.

After dark, Forsyth sent Jack Stilwell and Pierre Trudeau out, hoping they could slip through the ring of Indians and reach Fort Wallace for help.

During the night Sig crawled to his dead horse for some plums he had picked earlier and put in his saddle bags. As he groped in the sand he was shocked to feel the cold hand of a dead friend, William Wilson.

Two nights later, as he picked more plums from a thicket on the island, Sig passed the wounded doctor, still alive and moaning pitifully. Sig put a plum in the doctor's mouth. He saw the plum the next morning, still in the mouth of the doctor, now dead.

Early in the battle, Indian women and children watched from bluffs to the north. They shouted their encouragement to the warriors, and waited to strip the fallen enemy for valuables. But after four days of battle, most of the Indians rode away. Enough did remain, watching their enemy die slow deaths, that the scouts could not get out to hunt game.

Silent sentinels on distant bluffs constantly reminded the besieged scouts that they all might starve before their wounded died from lack of medical care. The rotten stench of horses and mules hung in a thick pall over the miserable men. All they had to eat was the putrid meat cut from those carcasses.

Sig Schlesinger continued to pick through the plum thicket, bringing in what fruit he could. On the fifth day, he shot a coyote and dragged it in before the watching Indians could stop him. He boiled the animal, including the bones and hide, and the men enjoyed the fresh meat and broth.

On the ninth day, a patrol of the 10th Cavalry rode up; the messengers had made it through! The next day more troops arrived, surprised that after nine days without rations, medicine, or reinforcements, any scouts still lived.

Forsyth wrote about his experience. He included this short poem about the young Jewish boy from New York who went west to find adventure and see the world:

When the foe charged on the breastworks
With the madness of despair,
And the bravest souls were tested,
The little Jew was there.

When the weary dozed on duty
Or the wounded needed care,
When another shot was called for,
The little Jew was there.

With the festering dead around them,
Shedding poison in the air,
When the crippled chieftan ordered,
The little Jew was there.

After its rescue, the company of scouts was brought back up to strength. It made two unexciting campaigns with the 10th Cavalry. Schlesinger then resigned and returned to New York, satisfied that he had seen the West, if not the world.

Suggested reading: Dee Brown, *Action at Beecher Island* (Garden City: Doubleday, 1967).

YOUNG IN YEARS, OLD IN SKILL

In spite of his youth, 19-year-old Jack Stilwell was one of Forsyth's leaders at the Battle of Beecher Island. When darkness and cold rain ended the first day's battle, Forsyth asked if anybody was willing to try slipping through seven hundred Indians and reach Fort Wallace for help.

"I'll try it if you'll let me pick a man to go with me," Jack said.

Forsyth thanked him for his bravery, reminded him that it was almost certain death, and asked if he understood the risk.

"Pierre, will you go?" Jack asked.

Frenchman Pierre Trudeau, one of the oldest scouts, had been a trapper and Indian fighter. He wore greasy buckskins and spoke poor English. He made up for his diminished vocabulary with increased profanity.

"By damn if Jack go, old Pierre go, you bet."

"You've got your men, major," Jack said.

Forsyth made a map, describing his position as best he could. Jack folded it and placed it in his pocket, as he looked around at grim comrades on what appeared to be a bloody island of death.

The Indians were resting quietly in their camps on each side of the creek, but the scouts could see that several warriors carefully watched the island. Stilwell and Trudeau wrapped themselves in blankets to look like Indians, slung their boots around their necks, said goodbye to the others, and slinked toward the creek. They moved backward down the creek bed in their stocking feet, so Indians, seeing their tracks the next day, would not be alarmed.

After they moved out of the creek bed, Jack and Pierre avoided hollows and ravines, realizing that the Indians would be less likely to look for them on open ground. Several times, small parties of Indians passed near, and they could hear conversations and the breathing of horses.

They had crawled three miles by daylight, when they hid in tall grass for the day. They could hear gunfire all day long.

When night fell again, their luck held, and clouds obscured the moon and stars. They continued southeast and soon met Indians moving from their village to the battleground. Fortunately, the mounted Indians could be seen in time to hide in the shadows.

When dawn came the scouts were dismayed to learn

that they were within a half mile of the village. But they hid all day in a swamp, as Indians occasionally rode past them in both directions.

Shortly after dark they waded the south fork of the Republican River and traveled all night without incident. Thinking they were finally away from the Indians, they decided to travel all day and reach Fort Wallace sooner. But at seven that morning they saw the advance guard of a Cheyenne village also moving south. Looking around in desperation, they found a buffalo carcass which had been killed the winter before. The ribs still had enough hide to form a shelter. They crawled inside   and spent the day watching the village pass.

They traveled as fast as they could the next night, running into snow at daybreak. They kept moving, and, about noon, reached a wagon road, fifteen miles west of the fort. They hurried on, having traveled all night and most of the day when the reached the fort.   They had traveled over one hundred miles from their besieged comrades.

Colonel Bankhead's relief command of one hundred men rode out before daylight.   Stilwell and Trudeau, both with very sore feet, were allowed to ride in a wagon.

Trudeau never recovered from the strain of the journey and died the next spring.

Stilwell continued to scout for Generals George Custer, Nelson Miles, and Ranald Mackenzie for the next thirteen years. In 1882, learning that his brother Frank had been shot to death by Wyatt Earp in Arizona, Jack went west, bent on revenge. But when he learned the facts about the killing, Jack changed his mind and turned around.

Stilwell became a deputy U. S. Marshal in Indian Territory. He studied law, and upon admission to the bar, became a U. S. Commissioner.

A good friend of Buffalo Bill, Stilwell moved to Cody's ranch in Cody, Wyoming, where he died in 1908.

Suggested reading: George A. Forsyth, *Thrilling Days in Army Life* (Lincoln: Univ. of Neb. Press, 1994).

OH, FOR A THOUSAND TONGUES TO SING

Major Forsyth, unsure that Stilwell and Trudeau had got through the encircling Indians, decided to send out another pair on the second night of the Beecher Island battle. He chose Allison J. Pliley and Chauncey Whitney. They tried, but had to return, finding the Indians had closed off every possible escape route.

The next night Forsyth, more sure now that Stilwell and Trudeau had not made it, sent Pliley and Jack Donovan. Pliley was glad Donovan got selected; he thought his partner on the first attempt was too fat to make the hazardous trip.

The two men took moccasins off dead Indians and put them on their feet. But unfortunately they did not, like Stilwell and Trudeau, carry their boots around their necks. So by morning, when they holed up in a buffalo wallow, thorns had punctured the wet moccasins like pins in a cushion, and every step was torture. They lay in the wallow all day, with no water and nothing to eat but the rotten horsemeat they were carrying.

About three the next afternoon, they saw a band of about twenty-five Indians riding directly toward them. It looked like the Indians would be upon them in ten minutes. Donovan, a Canadian by birth, was jovial to friends, always light hearted. He could sit at a campfire and sing songs all evening, never singing the same one twice. Pliley had a distinguished military career as an officer in the Kansas Cavalry both during the Civil War and later, after his scouting experience. He was known as a man totally without fear, which some thought came from his belief in predestination. He thought he would die when his number came up and not before.

One might wonder what different thoughts these two men had as they lay there, their rifles at their sides, watching the Indians ride toward them. But about a quarter mile away, the Indians stopped, talked a while, and rode off to the northwest, without seeing the scouts. At that point, Donovan let out a long sigh and softly sung the first line from a well known Christian hymn, "Oh, for a thousand tongues to sing."

Footsore and famished for water, they continued their weary walk after dark. At midnight they reached the south fork of the Republican where they spent an hour drinking and bathing their swollen, painful feet.

Every hour added more thorns to their feet and more

ALLISON PLILEY

Kansas State Historical Society

infection and pain from the thorns already there. But thoughts of their comrades, facing death from starvation and untreated wounds, kept them going. At three in the morning, on their fourth night of travel, they reached a ranch on the stage road from Denver to Fort Wallace. Exhausted, sick from eating putrid horse meat, and with their feet swollen to twice normal size and festered with thorns, they asked for food, a little whiskey, a bed, and a six o'clock wake-up call for the stage.

The rancher obliged, and they reached Fort Wallace, shortly after Colonel Bankhead had led his relief command out with Stilwell and Trudeau guiding. The fort, now down to one officer and a few men, got four volunteers from Pond Creek to ride with Donovan, who wanted to catch up with Bankhead. Pliley got a horse and rode out in search of a 2nd Cavalry detachment under Major James Brisbin which was patrolling out of Fort Sedgwick and thought to be in the area. After finding Brisbin and telling him about Forsyth, Pliley rode back to Fort Wallace to get treatment for his feet at the post hospital.

Donovan didn't catch up with Bankhead. By a great stroke of luck he found Carpenter instead, and led that command to the besieged scouts. They arrived thirty-six hours before Bankhead did. It was a good thing for Forsyth, too. The doctor with Carpenter's command said Forsyth could not have survived another day without medical attention. He had a high fever, and blood poisoning had set in. Forsyth probably owed his life to the determination and tenacity of Jack Donovan in getting to Fort Wallace and then catching up with Carpenter's command.

Donovan died in 1892, leaving a wife and seven children. After his distinguished military career, Pliley settled in Kansas City. He tried to volunteer for Custer's 1876 campaign, but he was unable to travel that far in time. His number didn't come up until 1917, when he was seventy-two.

Suggested reading: Arthur Chapman, "The Indian Fighters of the Arickaree," in *Harper's Weekly, July 26, 1913.*

FATHER AND SON

At 39, Civil War veteran Louis Farley was one of the oldest of Forsyth's scouts. He and his 19-year-old son, Hudson, were the two best shots Forsyth had. They and Barney Day had breech-loading Springfield rifles, not the Spencer carbines carried by most of the others. Louis and Hudson had homesteaded in the Saline River Valley, near present Sylvan Grove in Lincoln County, Kansas. They were two of the first men recruited by Jack Peate. Like many of the other scouts, the Farleys signed up with blood in their eyes. A few weeks before, Cheyennes had raided the Saline River Valley, killing Mrs. Farley and the other two Farley children.

When the Indians attacked and Forsyth led his scouts to the low island, he sent the Farleys across to the north bank of the main stream to take up sharpshooter positions. From their positions, seventy yards away, they overlooked the island below as well as the attackers across to the south. But the Indians could see them, too.

Very early on the first day of the battle, Louis took a shot in the leg shattering his thigh, and Hudson took one in the shoulder. Neither Farley said anything about being hit, and none of the other scouts knew it until the end of that first day.

Hudson thought he knew which Indian had shot his father. He drew a careful bead, pulled the trigger, and marked the place where the Indian fell.

The Indians moved away after the fifth day, and the scouts could wash in the creek and look for something to eat, besides rotten horse meat. The first thing Hudson Farley did was scalp an Indian.

When the scouts were rescued, they gave credit to the Farleys for killing the most Indians. Doctor Fitzgerald, who came with Carpenter's command, amputated Louis' leg, but too much gangrene had set in, and he died that night, the fifth victim of the siege.

Hudson Farley, now an orphan, claimed for the rest of his life that he had the scalp of his father's killer.

Suggested reading: Orvel A. Criqui, *Fifty Fearless Men* (Marceline, Mo.: Walsworth Publ. Co., 1997).

A COMMON GRAVE

The two scouts killed on the first day of the Beecher Island Battle were George Culver and William Wilson. Culver had served as an officer in the Colorado Cavalry during the Civil War. When Ottawa County, Kansas, was organized, he became the first county treasurer. Like the Farleys, he had homesteaded in the Saline River Valley. Nothing is known about Wilson except that he was a Confederate soldier in the Civil War.

Culver was digging in the sand beside Bill McCall when they heard someone shout, "If you fellows on the outside don't get up and shoot, the Indians will be charging us." Hearing that, both Culver and McCall raised up, looking for a target. A rifle cracked and a bullet grazed McCall's neck and flew on to strike Culver in the head, killing him instantly.

Not much is known about how Wilson got killed. One report said he was shot in the abdomen and died in great pain.

The two men were buried in the same grave, Culver below and Wilson above. Some of the scouts commented on the fact that the Union soldier and the Confederate soldier shared the same resting place.

Unfortunately they did not share it for long. When the detachment to recover the bodies came in December, they could not find the bodies of Beecher, Mooers, or Wilson. It looked to the soldiers that the Indians had opened the graves and removed those bodies. George Culver, buried below Wilson, escaped detection, as did Louis Farley.

Culver was re-buried at Fort Wallace. When that post was closed, his body was moved to Fort Leavenworth, where it was buried with full military honors.

Suggested reading: Orvel A. Criqui, *Fifty Fearless Men* (Marceline, Mo.: Walsworth Publ. Co., 1997).

MYSTERIOUS HEADDRESS

The first night's camp after the rescue of the Beecher Island survivors was made in an area where five tipis held burial scaffolds. One of them, made from white, freshly-prepared buffalo skin, obviously held the body of an important chief or medicine man. His buckskin headdress of eagle feathers was beautifully beaded and ornamented, with a polished buffalo horn mounted on the front. The headdress, over six feet long, was taken by scout Sig Schlesinger, along with other trophies.

The Indian had been dead for ten days, and the other scouts stayed away from Sig and his smelly souvenirs. But he had them washed by the time they reached Fort Wallace, and Jack Donovan offered fifty dollars for the headdress. Sig wouldn't sell, and the headdress was stolen that night.

The thief appears to have been Barney Day, a known mule thief before he joined Forsyth's scouts. Day had been seriously wounded in the battle, losing some fingers. Another scout said that Day claimed to have scalped Roman Nose, one of the Cheyenne's most famous leaders, who was killed on the first day. But other reports show that Roman Nose's body was removed by Indians before it could have been scalped. Sig Schlesinger always thought that the long body he had removed the headdress from was Roman Nose. The chief stood six feet, three inches. But most now think the body was that of Killed By a Bull, another Cheyenne, also killed in the battle.

Day had been a buffalo hunter, had much military experience, and was a crack shot. Some of the scouts credited him with a 1280 yard killing shot of a big fat Indian at the Beecher Island Battle. The Indian, out of reach of the Spencer carbines, had been insulting the scouts with words and gestures until Day set his Springfield breech-loader up on its shooting sticks and fired the fatal shot.

Day moved to Colorado in 1875 and became a county commissioner of Grand County. On July 4, 1883, he and the other two commissioners, plus the county clerk were shot to death in a famous gun battle involving the sheriff and his deputy, both of whom killed themselves later.

Many times in Colorado, Day had talked about and displayed a six-foot headdress and other trophies which he claimed to have taken at the Beecher Island Battle.

Suggested reading: Sig Schlesinger, "Scout Schlesinger's Story," in Simon E. Matson (ed.) *The Battle of Beecher Island* (Wray, Colorado: The Beecher Island Memorial Ass'n., 1960).

UNNAMED SCOUT

In his *Wild Life on the Plains,* George Custer described his firing of Joe Milner, chief of scouts, for getting drunk before the Washita Battle: "Thus ended California Joe's career as chief scout. Another was appointed in his stead." Custer never mentioned the replacement, Ben Clark, by name.

Clark was an outstanding scout. After the Washita Battle, General Phil Sheridan kept Clark on his staff as he led the follow-up campaign. Sheridan called Clark his "principal scout, the one who best knew the country."

Clark had left his St. Louis home in 1855 to become a 14-year-old courier at Fort Bridger, Wyoming. Two years later he became a teamster in Albert Sidney Johnston's Utah expedition against the Mormons. Then he served in the 6th Kansas Cavalry during the Civil War.

Ben Clark

After the war, Clark ran pack and wagon trains in western Kansas, and married a Cheyenne woman, by whom he had eleven children. His skill in the Cheyenne language, his understanding of Indian habits, and his varied frontier experience made him a valuable scout. Alfred Sully had hired him for the 7th Cavalry during the year Custer was suspended from duty. When Custer was restored to command, he kept Clark on as scout.

Custer probably refused to mention his chief scout by name because Clark disagreed with him.

Their relationship started out fine. Custer named Clark his chief scout on November 22, 1868, the day before they left Fort Supply, searching for hostile Cheyennes. Clark led the troops to the Indians' camp on the Washita River and scouted it well the night before the attack.

The next morning, Clark rode stirrup to stirrup with Custer as they swooped down on the unsuspecting Indians. When the bloodbath ended, 103 Indians, some of them women and children, had been killed, and fifty-three, all of them women and children, captured. Probably some of the captives would also have been killed, had Clark not intervened with Custer. One of the women the scout protected later became another of his wives.

After Custer's troops had burned the Indian tipis and supplies and had shot all the horses not needed to carry prisoners, Custer proposed to move back to Camp Supply. By then the scouts knew that they had attacked an outpost camp and that many more hostiles were camped downriver. In fact, it appeared that Captain Elliott's detail had engaged such downriver Indians and might be in need of assistance. When it was clear that, in spite of his officers' pleading, Custer would not go to Elliott's assistance but still intended to leave the river, Clark spoke up.

"You're asking your men to commit suicide," he insisted. "Those warriors from downstream will be all over you if you just ride away."

"And what do you suggest, Clark?" Custer demanded.

"Throw 'em off guard. Make it look like you're setting up camp to give your men and horses a little rest. Then make a feint toward the lower camps before you leave. That'll send 'em back to their own camps to protect their families. Give you a chance to get back to the supply train for more ammunition before they hit you."

Custer looked around. It was obvious the other scouts agreed with Clark, although the officers still wanted him to look for Elliott. Custer accepted Clark's advice, although he hated to listen to a civilian.

At dusk the bugle sounded, and the troops fell into place and made a feint down river. The warriors watching from high ground, left immediately for their own camps, and the cavalry turned and headed north to their supply train and on to Camp Supply.

Clark argued again with Custer on Sheridan's follow-up campaign. When they were unable to cross Whetstone Creek east of the Washita Battlefield, Custer proposed a twenty-five mile detour. Clark said he knew of a closer place to cross. Custer insisted defiantly that the scout was wrong. Sheridan, in command, took Clark's advice and found it correct.

Not once in his many writings about the plains, not once in his official reports, did Custer ever mention the name of Ben Clark, his chief of scouts.

Clark went on to serve under Nelson Miles in the Red River War, and under George Crook in the Sioux Campaign of 1876. General Sheridan said Clark was the greatest scout he had ever known.

In 1879 Clark married his second Cheyenne wife (not the one he saved at the Washita) and she also bore him eleven children.

Suggested reading: Wayne T. Walker, "Ben Clark, the Scout who Defied Custer," in *Big West*, v. 4, no. 4 (April, 1970).

A LITTLE GERMAN RIDES FOR HELP

In July, 1874, Colonel Nelson Miles commanded an offensive into the Texas Panhandle to force Cheyenne, Kiowa, and Comanche warriors back to their reservations. He chose Lieutenant Frank Baldwin as his chief of scouts. Baldwin promptly hired Bat Masterson and Billy Dixon, veterans of the fight at Adobe Walls, and others, including German-born William Schmalsle, a short, slight man, an expert shot and horseman.

Wm. Schmalsle

By late August, after initial successes against the Cheyennes, Miles was worried about his dwindling supplies. On August 31, he sent thirty-six of his wagons under Captain Wyllys Lyman to meet a train coming out from Camp Supply with fresh supplies.

Six days later and still worried, Miles asked Baldwin to lead a few scouts back toward Camp Supply and see what was holding things up. Baldwin picked Schmalsle, Ira Wing, and Lem Wilson. They left at dark on September 6.

By 4:30 A. M. they had traveled forty miles, and they knew the Indians were tracking them. The tired men decided to rest until daylight. The scout assigned to stay awake had to rub tobacco juice into his eyes to keep them open.

In a few minutes, the man on watch saw about twenty-five Indians approaching. He woke the others, and they held off the attack, but their pack mule ran off with all their food and bedrolls.

After daylight, the scouts mounted their horses and galloped through the encircling Indians. They spent the rest of that day alternating between galloping forward and stopping to dismount and shoot back at their pursuers. By late afternoon they had to stop for rest. Their horses were jaded, and for thirty hours three of them had had only a few minutes sleep, the other none. Fortunately a cloudburst came up and the Indians left during the night. They'd let some other warriors kill these stupid soldiers.

The scouts rode through rain the next day, avoiding another party of Indians, who were taking shelter under a creek bank. Ira Wing killed a buffalo that day and they had their first food, other than berries, since the pack mule had run away. Afraid to build a fire, they poured whiskey over the meat and ate it raw. Late that day, they captured a single hostile and kept him alive for questioning.

About midnight they reached an outpost of Lyman's returning wagon train. After turning their prisoner over to Lyman for questioning, the scouts had their first warm food for two days. At daybreak, Schmalsle stayed with the train to guide it back to Miles, and Baldwin and the other two scouts rode on toward Camp Supply.

Kiowas attacked the wagon train the next day, September 9, and held it under siege. The following day Lyman asked for a volunteer to break through the Indian lines with a message for Camp Supply that they had wounded soldiers and needed relief. Schmalsle, the little German who could ride and shoot like the best frontiersmen, stepped forward.

"I goes," he said.

Taking his pick of the soldiers' horses, Schmalsle rode out after dark. As soon as he broke away from the corralled wagons, the Indians raced after him in hot pursuit.

During the chase, Schmalsle's horse stumbled. He stayed in the saddle, but dropped his rifle doing it. The brave little German continued galloping forward into the darkness, staying ahead of dozens of yelling warriors.

Then Schmalsle came upon a large buffalo herd. He rode into it and let the milling animals obliterate his horse's tracks. He hid in the herd until the Indians left. When he rode out he knew he had a good chance of getting through, although he still had seventy-five miles to ride.

He reached Camp Supply safely. Within a few hours a relief wagon train, with Schmalsle back in the lead, started out on the ninety mile ride to the besieged train.

Lyman had lost two men and had several wounded by the time the relief train reached him. Most of the Indians had gone. The two trains moved on, soon reaching Miles with the much-needed and long-delayed supplies.

"Schmalsle, where the hell have you been?" Colonel Miles shouted, as the trains pulled into his camp.

"Mine colonel, such a story it is. I tells you after some sleep I get."

Suggested reading: Robert H. Steinbach, *A Long March* (Austin: University of Texas Press, 1989).

HEROES HERE HAVE BEEN

During the 1860s, renegade Indians said army scout Amos Chapman was the enemy they most wanted to kill. Chapman's toughest battle came in 1874. In June that year Kiowas, Comanches, and Cheyennes, bitter at the destruction of the southern buffalo herd, went on the attack. Seven hundred warriors battled twenty-eight buffalo hunters and merchants at the Adobe Walls trading post in the Texas panhandle.

After that attack, Indians continued to raid, pillage, and burn. Army troops converged from all directions. Nelson Miles, field commander in what would come to be called the Red River War, led four companies of the 5th Infantry and eight companies of the 6th Cavalry into the field. Chapman rode with Miles as his scout. Billy Dixon, who had fought at Adobe Walls, joined them as an additional scout.

Miles' command routed some Indians from the Palo Duro country, but the late summer heat and drouth exhausted his men and their supplies. Miles sent a wagon train out for fresh supplies. On September 10 the train was three days overdue. Miles had already sent other scouts out and heard nothing back, so he sent Chapman and Dixon to look for the train. An escort of three privates, Peter Roth, John Harrington, and George Smith, and Sergeant Zachariah Woodall rode with them.

They started at sundown, rode all night, and hid in a mesquite thicket the next day. From time to time they saw small war parties in all directions. When it was dark they started again, taking detours to avoid Indians. At dawn they were close to the train, but did not know that four hundred warriors had it under siege, a short ride ahead. The train had been found by scouts from the earlier group, but neither group knew that the other was so close by.

"Let's ride on to the Washita," Chapman suggested. "The cover in the bottoms will let us travel in daylight."

The men decided to risk it. They rode over a ridge and came face to face with a hundred twenty-five Kiowa and Comanche warriors. George Smith was detailed to hold the horses. The other five men tried to hold off the circling Indians.

Smith was shot in the chest. He fell, and the horses ran, carrying away all the canteens, bankets, extra ammunition and haversacks. Within a few minutes Chapman was shot in the leg, and the sergeant and another private wounded. The men crawled into a ten-foot diameter buffalo wallow, leaving Smith for dead behind them. Dixon carried Chapman, whose knee had been shattered, into the depression. As each man reached the wallow, barely a foot deep, he drew his knife and began digging deeper. By noon it was very hot and the men, all now wounded, suffered from thirst. Some had periods of delerium. Yet they kept firing whenever an Indian came close enough for a good target. In Chapman and Dixon, two of the best shots in Miles' army were in that shallow hole. Back at Adobe Walls, Dixon had shot an Indian from a horse at a range of nearly a mile. A growing clutter of dead horses and equipment where fallen Indians had been dragged away showed how the besieged men had taken their toll.

About three in the afternoon a storm came up and a cold rain fell, drenching the men. Pools of blood and water were two inches deep in the wallow, and the men lay on their stomachs and drank their fill. The Indians moved out of range for better shelter. Peter Roth went to Smith to get his pistol, rifle, and ammunition and found him still alive. Roth and Dixon carried Smith back to the wallow, but the wounded man died during the night. The survivors propped his body so the head showed over the edge, making the Indians think he was still able to fight.

Only Roth and Dixon were now able to move. Roth volunteered to go to Camp Supply for help. He started out after dark but returned in two hours, unable to find the trail.

The five men spent the night huddled together without blankets, shelter or food. Shortly after daylight Dixon started out for help. He soon met a detachment of 8th Cavalry troops from Fort Union, New Mexico Territory, under Major William Price. Price sent two soldiers and his surgeon to help the wounded men, but as they approached the wallow, the four scouts, supposing them to be hostiles, fired. They killed one soldier's horse.

Enraged that they had been fired upon, the surgeon made a superficial examination of the wounded men and returned to Price's column. More compassionate soldiers left some hard tack and dried beef. Not until midnight did Miles' wagon train arrive.

The wounded men were loaded on wagons and they reached Camp Supply on September 18, where they received medical treatment. Amos Chapman's leg was amputated just above the ankle.

All five survivors received the Medal of Honor. Apparently Chapman and Dixon were the only civilians ever to receive the medal.

After Nelson Miles became commanding general of the army, Chapman visited him every year in Washington. Four years after his amputation, he was back to scouting. He said the only difference was that now he had to mount Indian style, from the horse's right side.

"Amos Chapman was one of the bravest men I ever knew," Miles repeated often.

In 1925, a ten-foot monument was erected at the site of the buffalo wallow fight, about eighteen miles southeast of Canadian, Texas. It bears this inscription:

STAND SILENT! HEROES HERE HAVE BEEN
WHO CLEARED THE WAY FOR OTHER MEN

Suggested reading: William H. Leckie, *The Military Conquest of the Southern Plains* (Norman: Univ. of Okla. Press., 1963).

HIS FINEST MOMENT

Al Sieber fought in more Indian battles and killed more hostiles than Daniel Boone, Jim Bridger, and Kit Carson together. Yet he was highly respected and trusted by the Indians he fought. The finest moment of his remarkable scouting career came on March 2, 1875, when he walked into a hailstorm of bullets between two Indian groups at war with each other, raised his arms, and cowed the Indians into stopping their fight.

Born on February 29, 1844, in Germany, Albert Sieber was five when his widowed mother, following the lead of her oldest son, emigrated to America with seven of her eight children. The Siebers settled in Lancaster, Pennsylvania, Catholics in a community of Mennonites, Lutherans, Dunkers, and Moravians.

In 1856, this time following a married daughter and her husband, Albert's mother and her son, now twelve, moved to Minneapolis, Minnesota.

Minnesota was the first state to pledge troops to the Union Army, but a boy had to be eighteen to join. Since 1862 was not a leap year, Albert's birthday came on Saturday, March 1. Apparently the enlistment office wasn't open until Monday, because that was the day Albert joined the First Minnesota Volunteers. He was five feet, ten and one-half inches tall, with dark eyes and dark hair.

Fighting in the Peninsular Campaign, and at Antietam, Fredericksburg, Chancellorsville, and Gettysburg, the regiment became one of the most famous in the Civil War. During some of those battles the Minnesota soldiers carried an extra emotional burden, as the Sioux had taken the warpath back home in Minnesota. In a war which turned a boy's game, Capture the Flag, into deadly contests between armed men, the First Minnesota never lost a battle flag or a gun. "The First Minnesota doesn't run," became a popular slogan.

At the end of the Gettysburg battle, Al Sieber lay unconscious, his skull fractured from an artillery shell, his leg shattered by a rifle bullet, his regiment acclaimed as the one which stemmed the Confederate attack. "The heaviest sacrifice made by any single unit in one fight, during the entire war," it was said. Al lay in hospitals for five months. At war's end he returned to Minnesota and then moved on west.

He cut ties for the railroad in California, prospected in Nevada, and herded horses to Arizona, ending up in Prescott in 1868. After managing a ranch and going on two Indian-hunting expeditions, he became chief of scouts for General George Crook in 1872.

When the government herded Yumas, Mohaves, and Tonto Apaches onto Arizona's Verde Reservation in 1871, the Indians received the usual assurances about it being their home as long as rivers ran, grass grew, and hills endured. It was a beautiful land. With forty miles along the Verde River, extending for ten miles on each side, it was large enough that the Tontos could share it with their ancient enemies, the Yumas, as well as Mohaves, without too much friction.

But just four years later, in 1875, the rivers must have dried up, the grass withered, and the hills melted to dust, as the government decided to move the Verde Indians one hundred eighty miles east to San Carlos. Concentrating the Indians on one reservation would make them easier to control.

But the Tonto Apaches didn't want to go. Crook told E. Edwin Dudley, the former Indian superintendent for New Mexico whom the government sent to accomplish the removal, that it would be impossible. Crook did pledge the support of the army if the move could be made peaceably; he refused to use military force.

Dudley arrived at Verde in February, 1865, and tried to sell the government's idea to many hundreds of warlike Indians. Snook, a chief and one of the best men in Sieber's Tonto Apache police force, responded to Dudley's entreaty. He said he and his people would not go where they would be outnumbered by their traditional enemies. Their ancestors had died in this land, and the government had promised it to them forever.

Nevertheless, when the Indians were assured that the order came from General Grant, the Great Father in Washington, they agreed to obey it. The exodus began on February 27, as fifteen hundred unhappy Indians of all sizes and ages were herded along by a fifteen-man cavalry escort, plus Al Sieber and his Tonto policemen. Sieber put his policemen in the lead, which disappointed them as they didn't want their enemies at their backs.

The Indians well knew the hazards ahead of them. They would have to cross high mountains and ford swollen rivers. They had to carry all their possessions on their backs. Even the very old and the very young carried heavy loads.

One ancient Indian put his aged and infirm wife in a

basket with two holes cut in the bottom for her legs. Then he slung her up on his bent back, slipped a tump line across his forehead to support the cargo, and carried her the full one hundred eighty miles.

The cavalrymen walked, inviting the cripples, the children, and the weak to ride their horses. Some old ones died along the way. One day, two babies were born.

An intense snowstorm started the second afternoon, and the Indians were discouraged in that evening's camp. Dudley agreed to a short travel of only five miles on the next day, March 1. They went into camp early that afternoon, exhausted, muddy, frozen, and surly.

As usual the Tontos and the Yumas set up camp well apart from each other. Their ancient hostility rankled as their bodies neared the limits of endurance. Sieber could smell trouble brewing. A deer ran along a mountain near where the Yumas and Mohaves were camped. The excited Indians fired away, but the deer ran on, untouched. Sieber, grunting about such horrible marksmanship, picked up his rifle and dropped the deer with one shot. The Indians who had been shooting ran toward the fallen deer, but the Tontos, camped above, ran down and siezed it first. There was much grumbling that night in the Yuma and Mohave camps.

The next day the escort commander and the surgeon rode ahead to hunt, leaving Sieber in charge of both the escort and the scouts. The surgeon killed a deer and hung the carcass from a tree so the Indians could get meat from it as they came along. But, again, the Tontos took it all, leaving nothing for the Yumas and Mohaves.

Camp that afternoon was made in a pleasant valley, the pack train and escort farthest upstream, with the Tontos behind, and, further back, the Yumas and Mohaves together. Some Indian boys began playing on the vacant ground between the two Indian camps. After a time, they began to shout and taunt, and soon they were formed into two lines facing each other. Then Indian men began joining, and soon there were more men than boys, still in two lines facing each other. Then women screams were heard, "Kill the Tontos! *Kill* the Tontos!"

Raging warriors thronged to the ground between the two camps. Dudley tried to turn them back, but they overwhelmed him. People from the Indian agency dropped to their knees and began praying. Then Al Sieber, leading the escort, stormed through the attacking Mohaves and Yumas, who had begun shooting at the Tontos. He charged past the shooting Indians and into the center of the no-man's land amid the flying bullets. No one knows how Sieber, a few more scouts, and the cavalrymen

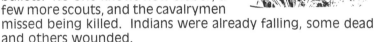

missed being killed. Indians were already falling, some dead and others wounded.

A general massacre seemed inevitable. Once it started, nothing would stop it. Warrors, women, children, and whites, as well, would have fallen. The casualties would have reached the hundreds. Only one man could stop it.

Al Sieber's career had been checkered. He was blunt and honest, sometimes kind, sometimes callous. On one scout he had taken an Apache prisoner, although his order had been to take no prisoners. He wanted to get information from the man, so he kept him around for several days, even though the prisoner was eating much of their short rations. Finally, as the scouting party breakfasted and the prisoner was eating his share, Sieber pointed his rifle behind the prisoner's ear and shot him dead. The packer said, "Al, if I knowed you was gonna do that, I woudn't have let him eat so much."

But on March 2, 1875, the man with the checkered career, the one man who could stop a massacre, stepped into his finest moment. He raised his arms in the midst of the enraged, furiously shooting warriors of three Indian tribes. His eyes blazed as the bullets whizzed past.

"Stop this now," Al Sieber roared.

And they did. It was too late for five dead Indians and many more wounded. But it was in time for hundreds more who lived — Apaches, Yumas, Mohaves, and Whites.

Suggested reading: Dan L. Thrapp *Al Seiber, Chief of Scouts* (Norman: Univ. of Oklahoma Press, 1964).

THE SIBLEY SCOUT

On July 5, 1876, eighteen days after the Battle of the Rosebud, General George Crook ordered a reconnaissance westward to look for the Indians that he had skirmished with in that battle. It is not clear whether he knew that in the meantime they had moved just eighteen miles west to fight Custer. He ordered two of his scouts, Frank Grouard and Baptiste Pouriere (Big Bat), to make the reconnaissance.

It would be hard to find two better scouts. Grouard, the son of a Mormon missionary and his Polynesian wife, had spent six years as a Sioux captive when young. When Grouard won his freedom he started scouting for Crook, who said he was worth a regiment of troops.

Big Bat was a half brother of scout Mitch Bouyer. General Crook considered Big Bat his most trustworthy scout.

Grouard preferred that he and Big Bat make the reconnaissance alone. But Big Bat said they needed a troop escort and Crook agreed, delegating Lieutenant Fred W. Sibley of the 2d Cavalry to lead it. Grouard said taking the 27-man soldier escort was the worst thing they could have done.

They started at eight in the evening, marching toward Fort C. F. Smith, intending to keep the Bighorn mountains on their left. They crossed the Tongue River the next afternoon, camping about three miles further on. The next morning they looked back and saw a Sioux war party of well over a thousand approaching the Tongue.

"My God," Big Bat said, "we're goners for sure."

Their only chance was to reach the mountains, where Plains Indians were sometimes reluctant to fight. They had a half mile lead when they started climbing, but some of the Sioux circled around to cut them off. Others stationed themselves at a canyon of the Tongue to prevent their escape that way. Shut in from all sides, their only chance, now, was to climb higher.

When they reached the place where Grouard decided to make a stand, everyone dismounted and they tied their horses where the Indians could see them as they approached. Grouard warned the soldiers to make every shot count or they would run out of ammunition.

The Sioux tried hard to draw fire and get the soldiers to expose themselves. By three o'clock only eight of the army horses were still standing.

The return fire began with one dramatic shot by Grouard.

He recognized Chief White Antelope and a warrior who, more daring than the rest, were riding very close, trying to draw return fire. Waiting until the Indians were lined up and taking careful aim, he killed both with one shot. The double shot confused the Indians, giving the besieged men about fifteen minutes to make their escape. They got down on hands and knees and crawled through the trees, then ran a mile and plunged into the Tongue River. Grouard put Big Bat in the lead, cautioning him to move from rock to rock, not touching the ground. The Sioux kept firing until dark, but never discovered where their prey had gone.

A terrible electric storm came up, but the soldiers kept moving until midnight. So many trees were falling around them that they took shelter under projecting rocks until the storm passed. Their only chance was to stay in rough ground where the mounted Indians could not follow. They crossed Wolf Creek about daylight. At times Grouard had to climb above the party, let a rope down, and pull the soldiers up. One time, Grouard led the party across a gigantic wall on a one-foot-wide path with a five hundred foot abyss below and a sheer two hundred foot wall above.

They came down from the mountains at the head of Soldier Creek and saw a large party of Indians who appeared to be waiting for them. But careful observation showed that the Indians had not seen them and were resting before riding out to engage Crook's main force.

The soldiers waited until sundown, when the Indians mounted and rode off to the east. During the night the party crossed Big Goose Creek, much swollen by the rains. Two soldiers, both non-swimmers, refused to cross and had to be left behind. The soldiers were now so hungry that they were eating baby birds, stolen from nests, feathers and all. Some of them didn't even bother to kill the birds first. Then Grouard found some Indian turnips, and the men filled up.

At ten the next morning they saw another soldier. Soon a detail went back for the two men left behind. They found them, unhurt, both sound asleep.

The Sibley Scout is one of the most miraculous escapes from Indians on record. Sibley had just graduated from West Point that spring. Very likely, an older, more experienced or brash commander might have refused to let the scouts take charge, thus getting the whole command killed.

Suggested reading: Joe DeBarthe, *The Life and Adventures of Frank Grouard* (1982 reprint by Time-Life Books).

FRANK GROUARD

Little Bighorn Battlefield National Monument

A QUIET MAN

Charley Reynolds, Custer's chief scout for the 1876 expedition to the Little Big Horn, had a badly infected right hand. When the 7th Cavalry marched away from the steamer *Far West*, Captain Grant Marsh, one of Charley's friends, begged him to stay behind. Although almost incapacitated, Charley insisted on going.

Reynolds, called Lonesome Charley, had few friends. He was a good man, quiet but not morose, cheerful and generous, but he liked to keep to himself. During his twelve years on the plains, he would show up at army posts, stay a while, then drift away, no one knew where.

Charley's hunting skill was uncanny. George Bird Grinnell, Yale-trained scientist, met Charley when he guided Custer's 1874 expedition into the Black Hills. They became close friends, and Grinnell described Charley:

"His quiet, self-contained manner, his gentleness, his bravery, and his wonderful knowledge of all that pertained to the hunting and war of his day, made Charley Reynolds a man to be remarked by all who came in contact with him. He was emphatically a gentle man, a brave soldier, a true friend."

The Indians agreed with Grinnell. Their name for Reynolds was The White Hunter Who Never Goes Out For Nothing. He could bring in game when even the Indians failed. They believed he had supernatural aid on his hunts.

Charley's father was a prosperous, very intelligent physician, and Charley had some college before he enlisted in a Kansas regiment for the Civil War. After the war, Charley went to Santa Fe, fell in love and married. But apparently he had too much mother-in-law, and he returned to the plains.

Charley was a peaceful man. He would never start a quarrel or insult anyone. But when an army officer attacked him, he fought back. The fight ended when the officer lost an arm.

Charley was about five feet, eight inches tall, heavy-set, and round shouldered. He did not smoke, and no one ever mentioned seeing him drunk. He was an astute student of nature, with keen gray eyes that missed nothing. He had a great knowledge of the habits of wild animals, which could only come from a long, intensive study.

One winter when he was providing meat to two army posts, Fort Rice in South Dakota and Fort Stevenson in North Dakota, he would tell other hunters that he would kill a deer or an elk, feeding on a certain kind of herb or vine at a certain hour of the day. Then he would go out and do exactly that.

Reynolds started scouting for Custer in 1873, when the 7th Cavalry moved to the northern plains. On the expedition into the Black Hills, Custer wanted to send a messenger through Indian-occupied country to Fort Laramie with the news that gold had been discovered. He asked for volunteers, and Charley stepped forward. Custer was reluctant to send a civilian through country bristling with hostile Sioux; it was a soldier's job. No one else volunteered to go, so he offered to send a guard detail with Reynolds.

Charley said, "No, one man has a better chance of getting through." Traveling by night and hiding by day, he reached the fort — one hundred fifty miles away — safely. But the intense heat and shortage of water almost killed him. His throat and tongue were so swollen that he could not speak when he reached the fort; his horse fell dead from exhaustion.

Three days after marching away from the *Far West*, Custer prepared to cross the divide into the valley of the Little Big Horn. Arikara scout Bloody Knife told the officers his gods had convinced him he would never see the sun set again.

Reynolds was also pessimistic. "Tomorrow will see the end of me, too," he said. "Anyone who wants my little outfit of stuff can have it now."

Reynolds rode with Reno across the river when Custer divided his regiment. The Indians attacked Reno's flank, intending to cut his command in two. Reynolds had a few civilian scouts with him as the soldiers galloped back to recross the river.

"Let's hold here, boys," Charley said. "Let's stop them so the soldiers can get back across." He was also waiting for Doctor Porter, then attending to a wounded soldier.

But there were too many Indians. They ran over Porter, then Reynolds. He had lost his rifle when his horse was killed. He used the animal for a barricade and continued fighting with his revolver. Over sixty spent cartridges were found by his body after the battle.

Lonesome Charley Reynolds was a quiet man — but a good man to be with when the going was tough.

Suggested reading: E. A. Brininstool, *Troopers with Custer* (Lincoln: Univ. of Nebraska Press, 1989).

A SCOUT'S WARNING

Mitch Bouyer, with a white mother and a Sioux father, grew up understanding the English, Sioux, and Crow languages. A protégé of Jim Bridger, he knew the country between the Yellowstone and the Platte rivers like the back of his hand. Some said he was the best scout in the army. Sitting Bull is reported to have offered a hundred horses for his scalp.

Bouyer was chief scout for the Montana Column, which marched down the Yellowstone to join Terry and Custer in the 1876 campaign against the Sioux and Cheyenne. When the columns met, Bouyer and six Crow scouts were transferred to Custer's 7th Cavalry. White Swan, Half Yellow Face, Goes Ahead, Hairy Moccasin, White Man Runs Him, and seventeen-year-old Curly volunteered to go with Bouyer.

As the 7th rode up the valley of the Rosebud, its flamboyant field commander leader took the lead, Bouyer on one side and Bloody Knife, leader of Custer's Arikara scouts, on the other. Three days later, Bouyer's six scouts reported many Indians in the valley of the Little Bighorn. In the dim light of the pre-dawn, they saw an immense herd of horses. Bouyer told Custer it was the largest Indian encampment he had ever seen. Custer laughed, saying it would be a short fight. Bouyer repeated the warning, and Custer accused him of being afraid.

"If we go in there, we will never come out," Bouyer said.

Bloody Knife looked up at the sun and bade it goodbye in sign language. "I shall not see you go down behind the hills tonight."

When Custer divided the regiment, he told White Swan and Half Yellow Face to ride forward to a ridge, look across the river, and see how big the Indian camp really was. Confused by Custer's attempt at sign language, they followed Reno's command instead. Bouyer and the other four Crows rode with Custer, as his command approached the river.

When Custer sent his trumpeter back to Benteen with the message to bring up the ammunition packs, Bouyer took Curly aside.

"Curly, you're young yet," he said. "You don't know much about fighting. I advise you to leave now. The Sioux have thousands more warriors than we do. We have no chance at all."

Curly rode away, and Bouyer and the other three Crows stayed with Custer. By now, the battalion was moving at a fast trot. Custer turned and told the scouts to go back and save their lives. Bouyer brought the scouts to a halt.

"You scouts need go no farther," he said. You have guided Son Of The Morning Star here, and your work is finished. Go back to the pack train and let the soldiers do the fighting."

The scouts wanted Bouyer to go with them. They reminded him that he was as much a member of the Crow tribe as they. His Crow wife, Magpie Outside, would be waiting for him with their two children. Just then Bouyer heard a Sioux yell, "Wica-nonpa (his name in that language), go back or you die."

"The Sioux have not forgotten me," he explained. "But I cannot go back." He remembered his mutual pledge with his closest friend, Tom LeForge, that if one fell in battle the other would look after the fatherless family. Tom lay in a field hospital, back on the Yellowstone River, unable to continue on the campaign.

As the three Crow scouts rode away, they looked back to see Custer galloping at the head of his battalion, his orderly on one side and Bouyer on the other. The three scouts joined Reno's command, just then beginning its retreat across the river from their heavy engagement in the valley. White Swan had been wounded in that engagement. Half Yellow Face had helped his tribesman escape.

Hairy Moccasin, Goes Ahead, and White Man Runs Him waited until dark and then left, circling the battlefield to go down the Little Bighorn. They met Gibbon's column and delivered the first news of the disaster. Curly was found a few days later as the Far West sped down the river with the wounded survivors of Reno's command.

But Mitch Bouyer, his body horribly mutilated by his Sioux kindred, was found on the battlefield with all the others in Custer's command. Bloody Knife was also killed.

Suggested reading: Edgar I Stewart, *Custer's Luck* (Norman: Univ. of Okla Press, 1955).

SCOUT AT THE LITTLE BIG HORN

White-Man-Runs-Him was born into the Crow tribe in 1858, somewhere near present Edgar, Montana. He had a normal Crow childhood. He got his name, replacing his birth name, at age ten. His father was Bull Chief, a famous warrior and chief.

A Crow boy had to perform four war deeds before he became a chief. He had to capture a horse from an enemy camp that was tied to its owner's lodge; he had to wrestle an enemy's weapon away from him; he had to count coup by striking an enemy with his bow or a coup stick; finally, he had to lead a successful war party — one in which no Crow was lost. White-Man-Runs-Him met the requirements and became a chief by the time he was seventeen in 1875. By then he was well over six feet tall.

The next spring he signed up as a scout with Colonel John Gibbon, who led one of the three expeditions against the hostile Sioux on the northern plains. Crows were faithful scouts for the army. They were glad to help punish their ancient enemy, the hated Sioux.

A scout's pay was sixteen dollars a month, the same that a private soldier got. Gibbon's scouts had thirty-two horses with them. To their great humiliation, a party of Cheyennes and Sioux stole every horse, shortly after the scouts signed up with Gibbon. What made this particularly galling was the Crow pride as the best horse thieves on the plains. White-Man-Runs-Him had a good sense of humor, so he took more soldier teasing about their loss of horses than the other scouts.

The scouts continued working on foot, keeping a sharp eye out for Sioux and Cheyenne horses. They gradually built their horse herd back up as Gibbon marched down the Yellowstone toward his rendezvous with General Terry and Lieutenant Colonel Custer.

Gibbon and Terry met on June 21 and made plans to find and attack the Sioux and Cheyennes. Those plans included transferring six of Gibbons' best scouts, with Mitch Bouyer as interpreter, to Custer's cavalry. Selected were White-Man-Runs-Him, Goes Ahead, Half Yellow Face, White Swan, Hairy Moccasin, and Curly, the youngest at seventeen. At eighteen, White-Man-Runs-Him apparently took charge, as he is the one most often mentioned.

Custer, who had brought Arikara scouts with him from

WHITE-MAN-RUNS-HIM

E. S. Curtis Photo from Author's Collection

Fort Lincoln, thought the Crow scouts were the finest looking Indians he had ever seen. Custer told the scouts that if the soldiers defeated the hostiles, the scouts could keep all the horses they captured from the enemy.

The six Crow scouts led Custer's 7th Cavalry up the Rosebud River Valley. On June 24, they passed the place where Sitting Bull had held a Sun Dance ceremony a few days before. Talking by sign with Sioux and Cheyennes in the distance, White-Man-Runs-Him learned that some big medicine had just been made at the sun dance. Both the Crows and the Arikaras studied the signs left at the hostile encampment, and predicted that the Indians would defeat the soldiers.

"If you follow the Sioux into the Big Horn country, they will turn and destroy us," the scouts warned.

By now, the trail they followed was growing larger as smaller bands had joined in. Custer sent White-Man-Runs-Him, Goes Ahead, and Hairy Moccasin ahead to see where the trail led. They returned, saying it was too dark to tell for sure, but they thought it went into the valley of the Little Big Horn.

"We have to know for sure," Custer said. "We can't let 'em get away. White-Man-Runs-Him, you take your scouts and follow all night, if necessary. We've got to find their camp."

White-Man-Runs-Him knew the land better than anyone. He told Custer about a place on the divide ahead where the Crows had often observed the valley of the Little Big Horn in their wars against the Sioux.

"How far ahead is it?" Custer asked.

"Maybe can ride in two hours," White-Man-Runs-Him said.

"Then you take your Crows and some of my Arikaras and ride hard to reach it before daylight. You can take army horses if you want. How far is this lookout from the valley?"

"Maybe twelve, fifteen miles."

"Then you'll be able to see their morning fires if they're there in that valley."

"Yes."

"I'll rest the troops a while and then we'll ride up closer."

The scouts reached the divide before three a.m., dawn in Montana Territory on June 25. White-Man-Runs-Him, Goes Ahead, and Hairy Moccasin climbed the lookout first. They could see morning fires from the hostile lodges, and so many horses they looked like maggots crawling on a buffalo skin, pegged down for scraping. Word was sent back to Custer, now ten miles behind them.

When Custer arrived, White-Man-Runs-Him warned that

he thought two Sioux riding nearby had seen the cavalry breakfast fires. Custer didn't believe his scout.

White-Man-Runs-Him, Goes Ahead, and Hairy Moccasin rode with Custer's five troops after Benteen's and Reno's battalions were split off. At Medicine Tail Coulee they were ordered back to the pack train.

"You've found the Sioux," Custer said. "Your job is done."

But when they met Benteen, he ordered the scouts to turn around and go with his troops, as they hurried to reinforce Reno. When they reached the Sioux, the horse White-Man-Runs-Him rode was shot and killed under him. The three scouts helped dig the entrenchments on Reno Rill.

After dark, White-Man-Runs-Him reminded the other two scouts that Custer had discharged them and told them to return to their village, their job done. The scouts also discussed that if the victorious Sioux now turned to attack the Crow village, the Crows would need every warrior they had. They decided to leave.

The three scouts, on two horses, soon ran into four Sioux. One of them rode a horse some distance from the others. Goes Ahead shot the lone Sioux. After they had their victim scalped and all three had counted coup, White-Man-Runs-Him caught the horse, and the three scouts rode on. The horse wasn't much — old with a sore back — but it was better than riding double, until the horse gave out and White-Man-Runs-Him was back on foot again.

The scouts had stripped before the battle, and the night was rainy and cold. White-Man-Runs-Him didn't mind the walking; it helped keep his blood warm. They skirted the Custer part of the battlefield and reached the Big Horn River, near present Hardin. They shivered until dawn, after the longest day of their lives.

After daylight, they saw Lieutenant James Bradley from Gibbon's command and some of his Crow scouts. After telling the terrible news of the Custer defeat, the three scouts were fed and given blankets for warmth. By noon Bradley had taken them to General Terry.

White-Man-Runs-Him had to tell the general four times before he would believe the words he was hearing about the outcome of the battle.

Suggested reading: Dennis Harcey & Brian Croone, *White-Man-Runs-Him, Crow Scout with Custer* (Evanston: Evanston Publishing, 1995).

LIFE WAS BORING AWAY FROM THE INDIANS

Tom LeForge lived enough in his eighty-one years for a half-dozen lifetimes. His family moved to Kansas when he was three, and Tom grew up with Potawatomi children. In 1864, when Tom was fourteen, his family moved to Montana to get in on the gold rush. When he was eighteen, he was adopted into the Crow tribe and given the name Horse Rider in recognition of his riding ability. He became a close friend of army scout Mitch Bouyer, who was half Sioux.

After Bouyer married Magpie Outside, a Crow girl, Tom often visited his best friend's lodge. There he met Cherry, a tall, brown-haired girl who often visited her best friend, Magpie Outside. It was love at first sight; soon Tom was sending gifts to Cherry's widowed mother. When Tom and Cherry married, the girl asked for a white ceremony with a ring, in addition to the traditional Crow marriage. Cherry would wear Tom's ring until her death.

Soon each couple had a son and a daughter. Tom became an army scout with Mitch. The two friends pledged to each other that if one fell in battle, the other would look after the fatherless family.

Mitch rode into the valley of the Little Bighorn with George Custer's 7th Cavalry. Tom had a broken collarbone and was left behind. In spite of his riding skill and his Indian name, his horse had pitched him off a few days before. Tom brought the news of Bouyer's death to Magpie Outside. He and Cherry tried to comfort her and the children.

But Cherry could not offer solace for long. She came down with a mysterious disease that neither the white doctors nor the tribal healers could cure. Finally she went to a hot springs where Indians said miracles sometimes happened.

But there was no miracle for Cherry. Before her body was wrapped and lifted to the burial scaffold, Tom's discharge papers from his latest campaign were folded against her breast. The papers and the ring would be proof in the spirit land that she was his wife. Cherry had always been proud of that.

Cherry told Tom before she died that she wanted him to marry her dearest friend and keep the two families together. Tom and Magpie Outside did marry, hoping they could forget their grief as they raised the four children together. Tom adopted Mitch's children, and they used his name for the rest of their lives. But Magpie Outside continued to grieve for her half-Sioux husband; she never understood the white one. Tom continued to scout for the army, but they let him go when he refused to serve against his friends, the Nez Perce. Then he tried ranching and mining. After ten years it seemed to Magpie Outside that her husband was becoming more "white" than Indian, and she was displeased. She missed the freedom and sociability of Indian camp life. One day she hitched her team to a wagon and loaded her belongings. She went back to the tribe, taking the four children with her. With this Crow divorce, she remarried a Crow Indian.

Tom drifted back to life as a white. He married a white woman in Montana and joined the circus. Then he settled down in a beautiful, mountain-circled valley, north of Yellowstone Park. His wife loved the valley, but Tom was still restless. He went west to prospect in Washington and Oregon. His wife, refusing to leave Montana, divorced him.

Tom married again in Washington, and he went to Alaska to hunt for gold. He returned to Washington and tried brickmaking and tie-cutting. But nothing seemed right. In 1912, at age sixty-two, Tom went back to the Crows, the people he had always loved. His latest wife refused to go with him.

Tom enjoyed visiting Magpie Outside and her Crow husband. But nothing had ever taken the place of the tall, brown-haired young girl Tom had loved so many years before.

Speaking of his second wife, Magpie Outside, he said, "Her love included all human beings. She was the special friend of every orphan and decrepit old person in the tribe. When she died, her husband and I mourned together her loss."

Magpie Outside had kept her promise and educated all four children. In Tom's later years he was always proud of his many Indian grandchildren and great grandchildren. Tom died at eighty-one, confident that he would find the spirits of his two Indian wives, still best friends, "together, always kind, always generous, always dispensing happiness."

Suggested reading: Thomas Marquis, *Memoirs of a White Crow Indian* (Lincoln: University of Nebraska Press, 1974).

FIRST SCALP FOR CUSTER

Buffalo Bill Cody was scouting for the 5th Cavalry out of Fort Laramie when news of Custer's defeat at the Little Bighorn arrived. The 5th was ordered to the Bighorn country immediately. On the way, regimental commander Wesley Merritt learned that eight hundred Cheyenne warriors had just left the Red Cloud Agency to join the hostile Sioux and Cheyennes who had defeated Custer. He hoped to intercept them on his way north.

The 5th made a forced march of eighty-five miles in thirty-one hours to a creek near present Montrose, Nebraska, arriving late on July 16, 1876. Cody was out scouting before dawn the next day. He found the Cheyennes a short distance southeast. By five o'clock the Indians were on the move, unaware the cavalry was already at the creek.

The regiment mounted their horses quietly and stayed out of sight. Cody and Merritt, with a few other officers, rode to the top of a hill and watched as the Cheyennes approached. Suddenly, about fifteen Indians rode rapidly to the west. Using their field glasses, the cavalrymen saw two soldiers riding along the trail they had followed the day before. The soldiers were apparently carrying dispatches. Merritt wanted to protect the two couriers, who were unaware the Indians were after them, but he hated to let the Indians know that a large cavalry command was waiting to trap them. Cody suggested that he take a few scouts and intercept the small party of Indians just before they charged the couriers. Merritt approved.

Cody rode back to the command, selected his scouts, and returned to the hill. When the couriers were about four hundred yards away and the Indians two hundred yards behind them, Merritt said, "Go in now, Cody, and be quick about it."

In a short running fight, the scouts killed three Indians and drove the rest back toward the main Indian party. Then an Indian, dressed like a war chief with a full-length warbonnet, rode forward and called out to Cody:

"I know you, Pa-he-haska; if you want to fight, come ahead and fight me."

The Indian rode his pinto back and forth in front of the other warriors, as though to badger Cody. Cody accepted the challenge and galloped his strawberry roan forward to meet the Indian. By then the Indian was also galloping forward at full speed.

Both men fired when they were about thirty yards apart. The Indian missed; Cody's bullet went through the Indian's leg and killed his horse. Just then, Cody's horse stepped into a prairie dog hole and fell. Both combatants were on their feet immediately, about twenty yards apart. They fired their rifles at the same instant. Again, the Indian missed; Cody's bullet struck the Indian's chest. Before he fell, Cody was upon him with his knife drawn. He jerked off the Indian's warbonnet, and scalped him.

Merritt sent one company forward to protect Cody as the Indians' shock gave way to rage. When the soldiers rode up, Cody waved the bonnet and the dripping scalp in the air and shouted, "First scalp for Custer."

Merritt, seeing he could no longer surprise the Indians, ordered the whole regiment to charge. They drove the Indians back to the Red Cloud Agency. While there, Cody learned that his duelist was Yellow Hair, a son of Cut Nose, a leading Cheyenne chief. Cut Nose offered Cody four mules for his son's warbonnet, guns, and ornaments, which Cody had captured. Cody refused the trade.

William Cody had killed his first Indian when he was twelve years old. He served in the cavalry in the Civil War. He killed over four thousand buffalo as a contract meat hunter for railroad construction crews. During a one- year period he was in more expeditions and Indian battles than anyone in the army. In one he personally killed Tall Bull, famed Cheyenne chief. He was the hero of countless dime novels, and for ten years he played in western spectaculars before audiences around the world. Some of the time, Sitting Bull was in the cast. Cody founded the city in Wyoming named for him.

But public acceptance of Buffalo Bill as one of America's most authentic heroes began on July 17, 1876, when he took the first scalp for Custer.

Suggested reading: Don Russell, *The Lives and Legends of Buffalo Bill* (Norman: Univ. of Oklahoma, 1960)

ORDERING INFORMATION

True Tales of the Old West is projected for 36 volumes.

Proposed titles include:

Warriors and Chiefs	In print
Soldiers	In print
Native Women	In print
Mountain Men	In print
Pioneer Women	In print
Ranchers and Cowboys	In print
Horses and Riders	In print
Miners	In print
Entertainers	In print
Dogs and Masters	In print
Outlaws	In print
Frontiersmen	In print
Gamblers	In print
Lawmen	In print
Scouts	In print
Homesteaders	Soon to appear
Vigilantes	Soon to appear
Writers	Soon to appear
Explorers	Under way
Courts & Lawyers	Under way
Railroaders	Under way
Merchants	Started
Army Women	Started
Children	Started
Duelists	Started

Ask at your bookstore or write:

PIONEER PRESS
Box 216
Carson City, NV 89702-0216
(775) 888-9867